The Art of Styling Sentences

20 Patterns for Success

Third Edition

by

Marie L. Waddell
formerly, Director of Composition

Robert M. Esch
Associate Professor

Roberta R. Walker
Associate Professor Emerita

Department of English
The University of Texas at El Paso

BARRON'S

Barron's Educational Series, Inc.

All inquiries should be addressed to:

Barron's Educational Series, Inc.
250 Wireless Boulevard
Hauppauge, New York 11788

Library of Congress Catalog Card No. 92-34542

International Standard Book No. 0-8120-1448-0

Library of Congress Cataloging-in-Publication Data

Waddell, Marie L.
The art of styling sentences: 20 patterns for success / by Marie L. Waddell, Robert
M. Esch, Roberta R. Walker. — 3rd ed.
p.   cm.
Includes bibliographical references.
ISBN 0-8120-1448-0
1. English language—Sentences. 2. English language—Rhetoric.   I. Esch, Robert
M.   II. Walker, Roberta R.   III. Title.
PE1441.W25   1993
428.2—dc20   92-34542
                                                                                       CIP

PRINTED IN THE UNITED STATES OF AMERICA

456 800 9876543

Contents

Preface   **v**

Introduction   **vii**

Suggestions for the Instructor   **ix**
    Sentence combining   **ix**
    Suggestions for teaching CHAPTER 1   **ix**
    Suggestions for teaching CHAPTER 2—the patterns   **x**

Suggestions for the Student   **xiv**
    How to get the most from this book   **xiv**
    Marginalia: to encourage deliberate craftsmanship   **xv**
    A paragraph analyzing a simile in poetry   **xvii**
    A paragraph defining a term   **xviii**

1   The Sentence   **1**
    What exactly is a sentence?   **1**
    Some helpful references   **5**

2   The Twenty Patterns   **6**
    Now let's make sentences grow...   **6**
    Compound constructions   **6**
       PATTERN 1:   Compound sentence: semicolon, no conjunction   **7**
       PATTERN 2:   Compound sentence with elliptical construction   **14**
       PATTERN 3:   Compound sentence with explanatory statement   **18**
    Sentences with series   **22**
       PATTERN 4:   A series without a conjunction   **23**
       PATTERN 4a: A series with a variation   **28**
       PATTERN 5:   A series of balanced pairs   **33**
       PATTERN 6:   An introductory series of appositives   **37**
       PATTERN 7:   An internal series of appositives or modifiers   **41**
       PATTERN 7a: A variation: a single appositive or a pair   **45**
       PATTERN 8:   Dependent clauses in a pair or in a series   **48**
    Repetitions   **52**
       PATTERN 9:   Repetition of a key term   **54**
       PATTERN 9a: A variation: same word repeated in parallel structure   **58**
       PATTERN 10:   Emphatic appositive at end, after a colon   **62**
       PATTERN 10a: A variation: appositive (single or pair or series) after a dash   **67**
    Modifiers   **71**
       PATTERN 11:   Interrupting modifier between S and V   **72**
       PATTERN 11a: A full sentence as interrupting modifier   **76**
       PATTERN 12:   Introductory or concluding participles   **80**
       PATTERN 13:   A single modifier out of place for emphasis   **85**

Inversions **89**
> PATTERN 14: Prepositional phrase before S and V **90**
> PATTERN 15: Object or complement before S and V **93**
> PATTERN 15a: Complete inversion of normal pattern **95**
An assortment of patterns **98**
> PATTERN 16: Paired constructions **98**
> PATTERN 16a: A paired construction for contrast only **103**
> PATTERN 17: Dependent clause (in a "sentence slot") as subject **or** object **or** complement **107**
> PATTERN 18: Absolute construction anywhere in sentence **111**
> PATTERN 19: The short, simple sentence for relief or dramatic effect **115**
> PATTERN 19a: A short question for dramatic effect **118**
> PATTERN 20: The deliberate fragment **121**

3 Sentences Grow   **125**
Combining the patterns—ten ways **126**
Expanding sentences **131**
Myths about coordinators **134**
A sentence with special emphasis: the periodic sentence **136**

4 Figurative Language in Sentences   **139**
Figures of speech **139**
Simile **139**
Metaphor **140**
Analogy **141**
Allusion **143**
Personification **145**
Irony **146**
Hyperbole and understatement **146**
Further reading **147**

5 The Twenty Patterns—In Print   **149**
"Tough Country," from C. L. Sonnichsen's *Tularosa* **149**
Excerpt from Arthur Schlesinger's *A Thousand Days* **156**
"Place of Sorrows," from *On the Road with Charles Kuralt* **160**

Appendix   **162**
Punctuation **162**
Suggested review questions **171**

Preface

The idea behind the twenty patterns—that students can learn to write by imitating patterns—grew out of our classroom experiences after we discovered that teaching by rules almost never will work but that teaching by patterns nearly always will. Actually, this approach is not a new one. The teaching of writing by the imitation of patterns goes back to the pedagogy of the Renaissance; it was a common practice in the schools of Elizabethan England; it was certainly a widespread method of teaching in America from colonial times until early in the twentieth century. Our literary history shows that most great stylists of English—Shakespeare, Bacon, Donne, Milton, Jefferson, Churchill—learned to create good sentences by imitating examples from earlier literary masters. Current novelists, popular essayists, and scholars in all fields, using as they do sentence patterns like the ones in CHAPTER 2 of this book, also reflect in their writing their debt to the past, to the early masters of English prose.

The validity of teaching by imitation, by patterns for sentence structure and punctuation, became evident as we watched our students improve their ability to write, once they had sentences to imitate. Like Topsy, this book "just growed." It grew with help from colleagues in our department; our students helped us learn just what patterns they needed most often to get style and variety in their writing; other teachers offered encouragement and helpful suggestions as our patterns increased from ten to the basic twenty. The book evolved still further as we presented these twenty patterns in an English journal, in a statewide meeting of college teachers, in numerous workshops, seminars, and classes for graduate teaching assistants planning to teach English composition.

In the years since *The Art of Styling Sentences* was originally published, we have seen much success with teaching writing by imitating or dissecting sentence patterns. This current edition brings more timely examples of the twenty basic patterns. In addition, we've included an expanded section stressing when to use a particular pattern, as well as new checkpoints and exercises, a more detailed section on punctuation with illustrations, plus a recent essay by Charles Kuralt.

Woven into the text are examples of how professional writers have used these patterns. At first, some of their sentences may seem intimidating; instructors must, therefore, carefully guide students in analyzing these unfamiliar structures that appear in familiar patterns. Some of the overblown sentences will give students a bit of fun in evaluating, and possibly even in revising, the extravagant and melodramatic prose of a few of these professionals. We urge all to enjoy seeing authors carried away with analogies and other figurative devices.

This third edition encourages analysis of and experimentation with the same idea phrased differently. As students learn the patterns, they will make fewer errors and also master the conventions of grammar and punctuation. Much of the instruction from earlier editions, however, appears again, as it continues to work in helping explain the patterns to anyone writing both in and beyond the classroom, in a business or professional setting. We have been encouraged that an edition is now available even in Taiwan. We're hoping that students will find new ways of being playful or serious, dramatic or forceful as they write. Above all, we want them to take risks with patterns they've never tried before, to claim authority for their individual style, and to develop their own voice.

We want to thank Gail L. Mortimer, Director of Literature at the University of Texas at El Paso, for her detailed and painstaking critique of our work. She gave us numerous insights about style, organization, and content, even pointing out problems we had overlooked in previous editions. At Barron's, we have appreciated the gracious and professional guidance of our editor, Linda Turner, in preparing this new edition. We would also like to thank Ruth Flohn, copyeditor. We are particularly grateful for her astute and detailed commentary; her suggestions made good sense and strengthened our presentation. Mary Mc Carthy Waight, Desmond Kilkery, and other reviewers have offered excellent, realistic suggestions. As Mary Waight has said, "Teaching in this manner—through pattern imitation—is a little like teaching itself: the rewards are many." But Pete Hamill warns us, "Writing is the hardest work in the world not involving heavy lifting."

Roberta R. Walker
Robert M. Esch

EL PASO, TEXAS
SEPTEMBER 1, 1993

INTRODUCTION

Almost anyone can benefit by learning more about writing sentences. You don't have to be a student to benefit from this book; all you need is the desire to write well. And you must certainly want to create better sentences, or you would not be reading this page. If you know how to write good, basic sentences yet find that they still lack something, that they sound immature because they have no variety, no style, then this little book is for you.

But if you want to write better sentences, how do you go about doing it? The answer is simple. You learn to write better sentences just the way you learn almost every other skill: by imitating the examples of those who already have that skill. You probably have already discovered that it is easier to master anything—jumping hurdles, doing a swan dive, or playing the guitar—if you are willing to practice imitating a model. Nowhere is this principle more obvious than in writing. If you are willing to improve your writing skills by copying models of clear sentences, then the following five chapters will help you to master the skill of writing well, with grace and style.

The whole is the sum of its parts

CHAPTER 1 reviews briefly what constitutes a sentence. If you don't understand the functions of different parts of a sentence, you may need a supplementary book with a fuller discussion of sentence structure. This chapter briefly reviews the various parts of the sentence, utilizing the traditional terms you will find in the explanations of the patterns in CHAPTER 2. Analyze the sentences in CHAPTER 1 until you understand their various parts.

Skill comes from practice

CHAPTER 2, the heart of this book, contains twenty different sentence patterns, some with variations. Study the graphic picture of each pattern (the material in the numbered boxes) and notice the precise punctuation demanded for that pattern; you will then be able to imitate these different kinds of sentences. The explanation under each boxed pattern will further clarify HOW and WHEN you should use that particular pattern; the examples will give you models to imitate; the exercises will provide practice. With these as guides, try writing and revising until you master the skill of constructing better sentences.

As you revise, take some of your original sentences and rewrite them to fit a number of these patterns. This technique may at first seem too deliberate, too contrived an attempt at an artificial style. Some of the sentences you create may not seem natural. But what may appear as mere artifice at first will ultimately be the means to greater ease in writing with flair and style.

Clear writing comes from rewriting

Your first draft of any communication—letter, theme, report, written or oral speech—will almost always need revision. When you first try to express ideas, you are mainly interested in capturing your elusive thoughts, in making them concrete enough on a sheet of paper for you to think about them. An important step in the writing process—in fact, where writing really begins—is revision, an on-going process. You must work deliberately to express your captured ideas in clear and graceful sentences.

Combinations lead to endless variety

CHAPTER 3 will show you how some of the basic twenty styling patterns in CHAPTER 2 can combine with other patterns. Study the examples given and described in CHAPTER 3; then let your imagination direct your own efforts at making effective combinations of the different patterns.

Analyze the sentences from professional writers to discover rhetorical subtleties and ways of achieving clarity, style, and variety.

Imagination is one cornerstone of style

CHAPTER 4 will show you how to express your thoughts in imaginative, figurative language. Study the pattern for each figure of speech described there, and then deliberately try to insert an occasional one—simile, metaphor, analogy, allusion, personification, hyperbole—into your own writing. Or you might experiment with an ironical tone. Try to be original; never merely echo some well-known, ready-made cliché. Create new images from your own experiences.

Understanding comes from analysis

CHAPTER 5 contains excerpts from the works of experienced writers who have incorporated in their paragraphs patterns like the ones described. Study the marginal notes that give the pattern numbers you have learned from studying CHAPTER 2. Then analyze something you are reading; discover for yourself how writers handle their sentences and their punctuation. Don't be afraid to imitate them when you write. You will, of course, find "patterns" (arrangements of words in sentences) that are not in CHAPTER 2 of this book. Imitate others as well as the twenty we present.

SUGGESTIONS FOR THE INSTRUCTOR

Since this method of teaching students to write by imitation will be new to some instructors, we hope this section will offer helpful and practical suggestions. For the new teacher, we want to anticipate possible questions and provide some classroom guidelines; for the experienced teacher, we hope to offer a fresh approach to an old problem: getting students to write papers that are not dull and boring for them to write or for us to read. The following pages contain some hints for ways of teaching the material in CHAPTERS 1 and 2. Additional pages addressed to students also suggest valuable ways for the teacher to present the patterns and other techniques to a class.

Sentence combining

Concurrently with publication of the first edition of *The Art of Styling Sentences,* a number of researchers developed a teaching technique quite different from the "imitation" method described in this book. Sentence combining, introduced first by John Mellon and later developed in the work of Frank O'Hare, William Strong, Donald Daiker, and others, is the technique of deriving from a number of sentences, usually short, simple, kernel sentences, a pattern for combining them into one or two longer sentences. Through this type of practice the student develops syntactic maturity. The result of this method is effective skill building; students' sentences have greater variety, appear more mature and sophisticated, and illustrate how writers in the same class, working with the same kernels, are able to transform them into many different types of effective communication.

Suggestions for teaching CHAPTER 1

As we said in the introduction to the book, CHAPTER 1, "The Sentence," does not pretend to be a complete discussion of sentence structure. The English sentence took several centuries to develop and is, as Sir Winston Churchill said, a "noble thing" indeed. There are entire books dedicated to an explanation of it; hence our coverage is minimal.

The main thing to do with CHAPTER 1 is to review with your class the important "slots" in the standard sentence—subject, verb, object, complement, modifier, and connector. Be sure the students understand the terms and the functions of each. Give them some class practice in separating subjects from verbs in their current reading. It is sometimes easier for them to find the essential skeleton of the sentence if first they cross out, or put in parentheses, all of the prepositional phrases (which are usually modifiers, anyway). Then let them discuss the differences between phrases and clauses, between independent and dependent structures, between declarative and imperative sentences. Never assume that students will be very adept at this kind of analysis. Guide them carefully with detailed explanations and many examples.

Suggestions for teaching CHAPTER 2—the patterns

CHAPTER 2, "The Twenty Patterns," is the heart of this book and contains enough material to keep your students busy throughout the semester as they incorporate the material into their compositions. Pace your discussions to fit your class; don't go faster than your students can master the techniques, and never try to cover more than three patterns in any one class period. Since there is a logical grouping and arrangement of the patterns, you may find it easier to go straight through from PATTERN 1 to PATTERN 20.

You will need to explain each of these patterns in great detail; you will also need to justify the rationale of the punctuation. Before you start with PATTERN 1, write some sentences on the board and review the sentence structure from CHAPTER 1. A good place to begin any kind of analysis is to have students put parentheses around all prepositional phrases, using anything from their current reading—a textbook, the sports page, an advertisement, lyrics of a popular song, or the label on a ketchup bottle, or a coke can! This is an effective exercise because prepositional phrases are nearly always modifiers and almost never a part of the basic sentence.

Now, with your class, create appropriate graphic symbols to use when you analyze and discuss sentences. For example, you can use a double bar (‖) to separate subject and verb in independent clauses, or brackets to set off dependent clauses.

1. Draw one line under the main clause (in this case, the entire sentence):

   The atom bomb ‖ exploded our old world and mushroomed us into a new age.

2. Dramatize what happens when there are two independent clauses in the same sentence:

   The atom bomb ‖ shattered our old world (into smithereens); it ‖ suddenly mushroomed us (into a completely new kind) (of world).

Draw a circle between the two independent clauses (which *could* be separate sentences); then explain that only four things can replace the circle:

a. a period, which would separate the clauses into two sentences;

b. a coordinating conjunction *(and, or, but, nor, for, so, yet)* preceded by a comma;

c. a semicolon, sometimes followed by a connective such as *therefore* or *however;*

d. a colon, but *only if* the second clause explains or extends the idea of the first.

3. Use brackets to set off a dependent clause, and clarify its function as PART of the independent clause; use a single bar to separate the subject and the verb in the dependent clause:

Marcie ‖ bought [whatever she | wanted].
(noun clause used as direct object)

[What Tatum | needs] ‖ is more discipline.
(noun clause used as subject)

The little children ‖ played [where the fallen leaves | were deepest.]
(dependent adverbial clause)

4. Use a wavy line under an absolute phrase:

The war being over at last, the task (of arranging the peace terms) ‖ began.

5. Use a circle around connectors and other nonfunctional terms.

Next, it might be fun to show that these constructions work even with nonsense words. Provide one or two examples, and then let students put their own creations on the board and explain them.

A bronsly sartian ‖ swazzled (along the tentive clath).

Yesterday I ‖ thrombled (down the nat-fleuzed beach) [where glorphs and mizzles | lay (in the sun)].

After this review, the class should be ready to tackle the first group of sentence patterns—the compounds. Each of them is really just two sentences in one, but you must make clear the vast differences that are possible. Now is the time to have the class really master the Checkpoints under PATTERN 3, which cover the differences in the three compounds.

For exercises beyond those that accompany the pattern explanations, consider these ideas:

1. Follow your discussion of particular patterns by asking students to write ten sentences of their own using the patterns you assign. Have students label each sentence with the number of the pattern in the **left** margin. *The advantage of this book is the control you have through the pattern numbers.* For subject matter students can draw upon their reading, hobbies, sports, and other interests. If for any given assignment the entire class uses the same topic or idea, have the students compare how many different arrangements of words can express the same idea, but each with slightly different emphasis or rhythm.

2. Use SENTENCE PATTERN 1, the compound with a semicolon and without a conjunction, to teach or to test vocabulary. In the first clause of the compound sentence have students USE and UNDERSCORE the given word; in the second clause have them DEFINE that word.

    EXAMPLE: Zen Buddhism is an *esoteric* philosophy; only the initiated really understand it.

    OR THIS VARIATION:

    The Greek root *chrono* means "time"; a chronometer measures time accurately. (See how much you can teach about punctuation in a sentence with this structure!)

3. Assign ten vocabulary words, each to be written in a different sentence pattern. Have students underscore the vocabulary word and label the pattern by number in the left margin. If students give the pattern number of the structure they are imitating, you can check the accuracy of their understanding of the pattern at the same time you are checking the vocabulary word.

4. Require students to have at least one different pattern in each paragraph of their compositions. Have them label each sentence by writing in the left margin the number of the pattern they are imitating. See "Marginalia: to encourage deliberate craftsmanship" (pp. xiv–xv) for more ways of encouraging students to analyze their writing as they improve their craftsmanship.

5. Have students collect interesting sentences from their reading and make a booklet of fifteen or twenty new and different patterns, with no more than two or three sentences plus analysis on each page.

They may simply copy sentences they find, or they may clip and paste them in their booklets, leaving room for a description (analysis) of each sentence in their own words.

6. Take a long, involved sentence from the assigned reading; have your students rewrite it several times using four or five different sentence patterns. (These revisions may have to contain some words that the original does not have.) Have students read these sentences aloud in class, commenting on the various effects thus achieved.

7. Point out the effectiveness of incorporating PATTERN 8 (the one with two or three dependent clauses) into a thesis or of using it to forecast main points in the introduction or to summarize in the conclusion.

8. Toward the end of the term, after they have mastered the patterns and know them by number, have students analyze some of their current reading, even from other courses. Have them write in the margin the numbers of the sentence patterns they find. (See CHAPTER 5 for two examples.)

9. Some of the example sentences for analysis are from professional writers; they are often convoluted and excessively detailed. Yet they can be springboards for discussion of such things as style, punctuation, sentence length, level and appropriateness of vocabulary, content, or even historical information.

SUGGESTIONS FOR THE STUDENT

How to get the most from this book

The suggestions and exercises below may seem too simple or too artificial at first sight, but if you make a game of playing around with words, of fitting them to a formula, you will certainly learn how to write sentences that have flair and variety, and that is a skill worth developing. A well-constructed sentence is, like any artful design, the result of sound craftsmanship; it actually involves and requires:

a. good composing or construction
b. appropriate punctuation
c. a feeling for the rhythm of language
d. an understanding of idiom
e. clarity of expression
f. recognition of the power of rhetorical arrangement

If you are not in a composition class, but are working alone without a teacher's guidance, the suggestions below will help you to get the most out of this book, so follow them carefully. Don't be afraid to copy a pattern and fit your own words into it. Remember that every great craftsman begins as an apprentice imitating a master. By following the suggestions below and mastering the patterns, you will increase your skill in the art of styling sentences.

1. Study one pattern at a time. Write four or five sentences that follow that pattern exactly, especially the punctuation. Go through all twenty patterns in CHAPTER 2, taking only one at a time, until you are confident you understand the structure and the punctuation. Practice, practice—and more practice: this is the only way to learn.

2. In every paragraph you write, try to incorporate one or more of these patterns, especially when you find yourself tending to write "primer sentences," that is, short, simple sentences having the same kind of subject—verb structure. Deliberately keep trying to improve the quality and arrangement of all of your sentences, whether they follow one of these patterns or not.

3. Think of something you want to say and then practice writing it in three or four different ways, noticing the changes in effect and tone when you express the same idea with different patterns and punctuation. You may not be aware of these changes when you read silently, so read aloud often to train your ear.

4. Analyze your reading material for eye-catching sentences, ones that you think have striking patterns you could imitate. (CHAPTER 5 shows you how.) Whether you are reading a newspaper, a magazine article, or a skillfully styled literary work, you will find many sentences so well written that you will want to analyze and then imitate. Underline them; learn the pattern. Or from your reading make a collection of sentences that you have especially enjoyed. Or keep a special notebook of new and different patterns that you want to copy. In short, look for unusual and effective sentences in everything you read and make a conscious effort to add those new patterns to the basic twenty in CHAPTER 2.

5. Use your computer and its software to practice brainstorming and to capture ideas. Save your drafts on a disk, as they may be useful later. Practice using Spellcheck, Thesaurus, and other functions as you edit. The computer will help you plan, delete, add, and rearrange as you write and revise.

Marginalia: to encourage deliberate craftsmanship

Analysis for themes

In every theme or paper you write there should be some goals, some design that you are trying to create. Marginalia can be a helpful guide for you, a way of checking up on what you are doing when you write. Marginalia, which, as the name implies, you write in the margin, will consist of words and symbols that indicate an analysis of your writing.

In early assignments, your instructor will probably be highly prescriptive. When you are told how many words, how many paragraphs, sometimes even how many sentences should occur within paragraphs, don't resent the detailed directions. Think about them as training in a skill. After all, athletic coaches and music instructors alike begin their training with strict regulations and drills, too. So follow all the "requirements."

Things to do

1. Highlight the topic sentence of each paragraph. Identify it by the label **TS** in the margin.

2. In the **left** margin of each paragraph, indicate the attempted pattern from the sentence patterns **(SP)**. Mark in the margin **SP 6** or **SP 9a,** for example.

3. Indicate a pronoun reference pattern in one of the paragraphs by drawing a circle around each pronoun and an arrow pointing to its antecedent. Identify in margin as **PRO PATT.**

4. Circle transitional words in one paragraph ("echo" words, transitional connectives, conjunctions).

5. List in the margin the types of sentences in one paragraph; use a variety of simple **(S),** complex **(CX),** compound **(C),** and compound complex **(CCX).**

6. When you master a new vocabulary word, underline it and label it **VOC.**

You might use a different color for each type of entry so that you can see at a glance whether you have incorporated all the techniques of good construction. These marks might seem distracting at first, but the results will be worth the distraction. A glance at the marginalia will indicate whether you understand the composition techniques being taught.

Why bother with all of this? Because it works. There is no better answer. You will come to realize that a theme must have a variety of sentences, that there must be transitional terms if the theme is to have coherence, that pronouns help eliminate needless repetition of the same word, that synonyms and figurative language give the theme more sparkle than you ever hoped for. Your instructors will like what they are reading; you will like what you are writing, and your grades will improve.

The following pages show two paragraphs written by a student. Note the marginal analysis and the effectiveness of the different sentence patterns.

A paragraph analyzing a simile in poetry

The Movement of Time

MARGINALIA

"Like as the waves make towards the pebbled shore, So do our minutes hasten to their end . . . ."

—*William Shakespeare,* SONNET LX

TS

In the first two lines of Sonnet LX, Shakespeare uses a simile comparing the waves of the ocean to the minutes of our life: "Like as the waves make towards the pebbled shore, / So do our minutes hasten to their *SP3* end . . . ." This line is inverted: that is, the subject "our *SP 11* minutes" is in the second line, and the comparison "like as the waves" is in the first line. The simile says, in effect, that "the minutes of our lives are like the waves *VOC* on the shore." The waves role endlessly, inexorably *SP1* toward the shore of the ocean; the minutes of our lives hasten endlessly toward the end of our lives. This figure of speech gives an image of movement. We can almost *SP 10* see time, like ocean waves, moving toward its destiny: *SP 16* the end of life. Just as the waves end on the shore, so *SP3* too our life's minutes end in death. Some words in the *VOC* simile have particular power: the word hasten conjures *a repeated SVO pattern* up a mental picture of rapid movement, of inexorable hurry toward some predestined end. The word towards suggests a straight, unerring path going without hesitation or pause to some goal. The waves move toward *repeated SP10* their goal: the shore. Our minutes move toward their goal: life's end. This simile is a very effective, picture-*PRO PATT* making figure of speech. It paints a mental picture of *SP9* movement and destiny. It suggests a very important fact *Repeat of keyword* about life, a fact we must remember. That fact is the truth expressed here beautifully by Shakespeare—life goes on forever toward its end, never slowing down or *Summary of TS with "echo" of quote* going back. Our lives do indeed "hasten to their end."

—Shawn Waddell

A paragraph defining a term

A Junk-man

TS
Order: General to Particular
SP4A

SP14
SP12

VOC

Metaphor

VOC
SP1

Contrast

SP9
Definition of TS

repeated word for coherence
Example

factual data

Contrast
VOC and two levels of diction

SP1

echo of TS for coherence

A junk-man in baseball is the most feared pitcher of all. Most batters go to the plate with the knowledge that the pitcher usually throws either curves or fastballs or knuckleballs in the clinch. From his view at the plate, a batter sees a curveball pitcher's curve starting off in a line seemingly headed straight for his head. Fortunately, just before making any painful contact, the ball seems to change its own mind, veering away to the opposite side of the plate. But after long and <u>arduous</u> practice, any batter can learn to anticipate or recognize a curve and be prepared for it. The same is true for a fastball that blurs its way into the catcher's mitt or for a knuckleball which seems to have trouble deciding where to go. A veteran batter can learn to sense the sometimes <u>erratic</u> path of either ball; he can feel some confidence when he has some idea of the pitcher's preferred ball. But he can be put completely off stride when he hears he has to face that most dreaded of all pitchers, a junk-man—dreaded because he can throw all pitches with equal effectiveness and surprise. This element of surprise coupled with variety makes the junk-man the most feared of all pitchers in baseball. For example, when Sam the Slugger goes to bat, he can feel more relaxed if he knows that Carl the Curve-man will probably throw curves about seventy-five percent of the time. The same is true for Sam when a well-known fastballer or knuckler is facing him from sixty feet away. On the contrary, Sam the Slugger loses his <u>equanimity</u> and is tied in knots when Joe the Junk-man grins wickedly across that short sixty feet from mound to plate; Sam has no way to anticipate what surprises may lurk behind that wicked grin when he faces the most feared pitcher in baseball.

—Shawn Waddell

CHAPTER 1

THE SENTENCE

What exactly is a sentence?

Like sign language, the beat of drums, or smoke signals, sentences are a means of communicating. They may express emotion, give orders, make statements, or ask questions; but in every case they try to communicate.

In most sentences there are two parts that follow a basic pattern:

Subject ‖ **Verb**

Occasionally, a sentence may be a single word:

What?   Nonsense!   Jump.

In certain contexts "What?" and "Nonsense!" may communicate a complete thought. "Jump," as you can see, has an implied "you" as its subject.

Now let's break up each of two very simple sentences into their two parts.

The bees are swarming.

bees ‖ are swarming.

The zebras stampeded.

zebras ‖ stampeded.

Try making up your own example following the pattern above; box the subject and the verb, and insert a pair of vertical lines between these two basic parts of the sentence. Only two slots are necessary—the S (subject) slot and the V (verb) slot.

Now let's add modifiers to the subject, to the verb, or to both. Note that you still have but two slots and need only one pair of vertical lines:

The agitated killer bees ‖ are swarming in the apricot trees.

The startled zebras ‖ stampeded the white hunters.

Combining the S slot and the V slot, you can construct the most common sentence patterns. Each one has a traditional name, describing its purpose and the task it performs:

TASK	NAME
A sentence may make a statement.	Declarative
May it also ask a question?	Interrogative
Use it to give an order.	Imperative
What great emotion it can express!	Exclamatory

As you add words to modify the subject and verb, you will create longer sentences, some with phrases, others with clauses. Quite simply, a *phrase* is a group of words containing no subject—verb combination and usually acting as a modifier *(prepositional phrase, participial phrase, infinitive phrase)*. A *clause* is a group of words containing a subject—verb combination; sometimes the clause expresses a complete thought, but not always.

INDEPENDENT CLAUSE	makes a complete statement communicates an idea by itself
DEPENDENT CLAUSE	modifies a unit in another clause does not communicate a complete thought may be a unit in another clause.

These two types of clauses combine to form various types of sentences; the most common are these:

SIMPLE	makes a single statement is an independent clause has only one subject—verb combination
COMPOUND	makes two or more statements has two or more independent clauses has two or more subject—verb combinations
COMPLEX	has an independent clause has one or more dependent clauses functioning as modifiers
COMPOUND COMPLEX	has two or more independent clauses has two or more subject—verb combinations has one or more dependent clauses functioning as modifiers

The subject—verb combination is the heart of each sentence you write. With this combination you can build an infinite variety of intricate sentence patterns. In analyzing, note that each new subject—verb combination will require a new pair of ‖ lines. Longer sentences may have only one S and one V slot with one pair of vertical lines. Sometimes there will be only *one* subject in the S slot; sometimes there will be *two or more* subjects, all in the same S slot, because they precede the vertical lines separating S from V. Similarly, the verb slot may have one verb or several verbs.

Elizabeth and Mary Tudor ‖ were sisters but hated each other.

NOTE: Throughout this chapter one line will underline a subject; two lines, a verb.

Sentences often have an added attraction—something after the verb that is neither a modifying word nor a phrase—yet even these sentences may have but one S and one V slot. If the verb is transitive, you will find a direct object following it. A transitive verb describes an action that the subject performs—in the examples below, Ben's forgetting or Agnes's ignoring and continuing. A direct object receives the action of the verb and answers the questions "what?" or "whom?" Each of the following examples (both simple sentences) has one or more direct objects.

EXAMPLES: Ben ‖ forgot his galoshes.
DO

Agnes ‖ ignored her teacher's glares and continued her
DO   **DO**
mischief-making.

If the verb is linking, however, there may be subject completers (subject complements). A subject complement may be either a noun, a pronoun, or an adjective that renames or describes the subject. The following sentences illustrate the single S—V combination with one or more subject complements. Both sentences have *being* verbs *(am, is, are, was, were, be, being, been)*. Other linking verbs are *appear, seem, become,* and verbs of sensation *(feel, taste,* etc.).

EXAMPLES: Anne Boleyn ‖ was Henry VIII's second wife.
SC

Bargain basement sales ‖ may be _____ or

_____, _____ or _____, _____ or

_____.

(YOU *try filling in the blanks above!)*

To almost every part of the sentence you may add modifying words and phrases. You may retain the single subject—verb combination or else expand your sentence to include several subject—verb combinations, all having modifiers. Distinguish main clauses by putting ‖ between the S and the V in a main clause and ∣ between the S and the V in dependent clauses; then put brackets around dependent clauses

> EXAMPLES: Long or short <u>sentences</u> ‖ <u>can</u> sometimes <u>communicate</u> effectively the most difficult ideas in the world. (simple)
>
> Sterling <u>silver</u> [<u>that</u> ∣ <u>may cost</u> $800 a place setting] and small kitchen <u>appliances</u> like can openers or toasters [<u>that</u> ∣ <u>are</u> <u>considered</u> too basic] ‖ <u>are</u> no longer popular wedding gifts. (complex)

Now let's break a whole sentence into its parts. When making a mechanical analysis of any sentence, use the following labels to identify the various parts:

S	subject	**C**	connector (conjunction)	**M**	modifier
V	verb	**O**	object of preposition	**IO**	indirect object
			object of infinitive	**OC**	object complement
SC	subject complement	**P**	preposition	**DO**	direct object

The following sentence illustrates the type of analysis you might practice:

  M   **M**   **M**   **S**   **V**   **M**   **SC**   **P M**

The rundown, dirty shoes appeared unbelievably incongruous on the

O

model.

The following chapters will help you write more effective sentences and will give you clues to spice up dreary prose. Sentences come to life as a writer plans them; in fact, very few fine sentences are spontaneous. The following pages have models to imitate and use. The patterns presented are basic, but by no means are they the only ones. As your writing matures, you will discover additional patterns. As you master the ability to analyze and to compose sentences, you will be justifiably proud of your improving style.

And now you're off . . . on the way to creating better sentences, more polished paragraphs.

Some helpful references

For detailed information, materials, and examples of sentences, you may wish to consult one of the following recent publications:

Bizzell, Patricia et al. *The Bedford Bibliography for Teachers of Writing*. 3rd ed. Boston: St. Martin's, 1991 (free to instructors).

Hacker, Diana. *A Writer's Reference,* 2nd ed. Boston: St. Martin's, 1992.

Hairston, Maxine, and John J. Ruszkiewicz. *The Scott, Foresman Handbook for Writers*. 3rd ed. New York: Harper Collins, 1993.

Kolln, Martha. *Rhetorical Grammar. Grammatical Choices, Rhetorical Effects*. New York: Macmillan, 1991.

——. *Understanding English Grammar.* 3rd ed. New York: Macmillan, 1990.

Reid, Stephen. *The Prentice Hall Handbook for College Writers*. Englewood Cliffs, NJ: Prentice Hall, 1989.

Somers, Nancy, and Linda Simon. *The Harper Collins Guide to Writing*. New York: Harper Collins, 1993.

Strong, William. *Creative Approaches to Sentence Combining*. Urbana, IL: National Council of Teachers of English, 1986.

Troyka, Lynn Quitman. *Simon & Schuster Handbook for Writers,* 2nd ed. Englewood Cliffs, NJ: Prentice Hall, 1990.

——. *Concise Handbook*. rev. ed. Englewood Cliffs, NJ: Prentice Hall, 1992.

CHAPTER 2

THE TWENTY PATTERNS

Now let's make sentences grow . . .

This chapter introduces you to twenty basic patterns, which writers frequently use to give their style flair and variety. These patterns will not be new to you; you've already seen them many times in things you've read. Perhaps you have never thought about analyzing them, or realized they could help you perk up your own writing. But they can.

Study them. Why not give them a chance to help you?

Compound constructions

In CHAPTER 1 you studied the most elementary kinds of sentences. The easiest way to expand this basic pattern is simply to join two short complete statements (simple sentences) and thereby make a compound sentence. When you do this, however, be sure to avoid two pitfalls of the compound sentence:

a. the fused or run-on sentence (which has no punctuation between the two sentences that have been joined);

b. the comma splice (which has a mere comma instead of a period, semicolon, or colon to separate the two sentences you have joined).

A comma between independent clauses must precede *and, but, or, yet, so, nor,* or *for.* Of course, you will have no trouble avoiding these two pitfalls if you faithfully copy the following patterns for compound sentences, being careful to imitate the punctuation exactly.

COMPOUND SENTENCE: SEMICOLON,
NO CONJUNCTION
(two short, related sentences now joined)

S   V   ;   S   V   .

EXPLANATION:

This pattern helps you join two short, simple sentences having two closely related ideas. Simply use a semicolon instead of a conjunction with a comma. The graphic illustration in the box above and the examples below show only two clauses; you may, of course, have three or more.

And remember the definition of a complete clause: a subject—verb combination that makes a full statement. In other words, an independent clause must have a finite verb; therefore look for one that suggests completed action on each side of the semicolon. Remember that what precedes and what follows the semicolon (PATTERN 1) must be capable of standing alone.

This is a fragment:

> The reason for the loss in yardage being
> the broken shoe-string on the left guard's shoe.

Being is the wrong verb form; change it to *was* and make a sentence.

This is another kind of fragment:

> Which was the only explanation that he could give at that
> moment.

This fragment is a dependent clause, in spite of the subject—verb combinations (*which was* and *he could give*), because of the subordinating word (in this case, a relative pronoun) at the beginning. Remember this equation:

Because
If
When   }   +   a subject—verb   =   a fragment
After   (plus)   combination   (equals)   every time.
and other such sub-
ordinating words

These are common semicolon errors:

> For example ; . . . .

> Because the snow was deep and the temperature below zero ; . . . .

> The work having been finished by five o'clock ; . . . .

✔ These three errors can be corrected thus:

For example, ...

Because the snow was deep, the temperature fell below zero.
The work was finished by five o'clock.

✔ In short, don't confuse commas and semicolons.

When to use this pattern

This pattern will help you when you've talked about a number of similar ideas in several sentences. You combine these ideas into a single, more powerful sentence that conveys the information you've previously expressed in three or four sentences. During revision you should look for paragraphs with too many short sentences with parallel ideas and ask yourself, "Can I combine these sentences to give my message a more forceful impact?"

EXAMPLES:

Caesar, try on this toga; it seems to be your size.

Hard work is only one side of the equation; talent is the other.

Some people dream of being something; others stay awake and are.

Human beings are related to the monkey; only a monkey, however, would ever admit the relationship.

HOW PROFESSIONALS HANDLE THE PATTERN:

Throughout this book are many professional examples for analysis. Study them to see how experienced writers handle (or mishandle) the various patterns. Look for ways these authors manipulate word order and punctuation to convey their message. Note how they create interest through sentence variety. At times you'll find an example questionable, as if the writer let style rule sense. Don't be afraid to imitate, praise, or attack these examples.

"E. T., don't phone home; it's too expensive." —*El Paso Herald-Post*

"Singapore has 11,910 people per square mile; Mongolia has only three." —*Condé Nast Traveler*

"By day, there's the constant threat of collision; by night, armed robbers scatter nails or block the road with rocks."—Constance Bond, *Smithsonian,* May 1992

"Be content with your lot; one cannot be first in everything." —Aesop

"As a hero in Celtic mold, he must be fitted for the warrior's paradise; as a hero in Christian terms, he must win entry to Heaven."—Graeme Fife, *Arthur the King*

(Note the parallelism in the two clauses.)

"It is not going to be one big party; it is not going to be fireworks and cakes."—*European Travel and Life*

(Note the parallel negatives here.)

"Forget defensive driving; practice paranoid driving."—Jim Lanham, *El Paso Herald-Post*

VARIATIONS:

Pattern 1a

The first variation, PATTERN 1a, involves the use of conjunctive adverbs (connectors) such as *however, hence, therefore, thus, then, moreover, nevertheless, likewise, consequently,* and *accordingly.*

The use of a comma after the connector is optional.

$$\underline{\quad S \quad \quad V \quad}; \text{however,} \underline{\quad S \quad \quad V \quad}.$$

EXAMPLES: David had worked in the steaming jungle for two years without leave; hence he was tired almost beyond endurance.

This gadget won't work; therefore there is no sense in buying it.

Pattern 1b

For the second variation, PATTERN 1b, use a coordinating conjunction (also a connector) such as *and, or, for, but, nor, yet,* or *so.*

$$\underline{\quad S \quad \quad V \quad}; \underline{\quad S \quad \quad V \quad}, \text{and} \underline{\quad S \quad \quad V \quad}.$$

$$\underline{\quad S \quad \quad V \quad}, \text{but} \underline{\quad S \quad \quad V \quad}; \underline{\quad S \quad \quad V \quad}.$$

EXAMPLES: It was snowing outside, and in the building Harold felt safe; he dreaded leaving his shelter for the long, dangerous trip home.

It was radical; it was daring, but mostly it was cheap.

Some people blamed the judge; others blamed the defendants, and still others blamed all parties to the trial of the political prisoners, which from almost any viewpoint was a disgrace to American justice.

"They [the Tarahumara Indians] are also undoubtedly the greatest natural runners on earth; they call themselves Rara muri, 'The Runners,' or 'The Running People,' and there are many tales of their prowess on foot." —Rob Schultheis, "Into a Canyon, Back in Time," *National Geographic Traveler,* September/October 1992.

The squirrel in our front yard is a playful sort; he mocks us from his tree, but I can entice him from his treetop home with a few crusts of bread.

Pattern 1c

Try this third variation, PATTERN 1c:

$$\underline{\quad S \quad\quad V \quad} ; \underline{\quad S \quad\quad V \quad} ; \underline{\quad S \quad\quad V \quad} .$$

EXAMPLES: North bid one club; East passed; South bid one spade; West doubled.

"To spend too much time in studies is sloth; to use them too much for ornamentation is affectation; to make judgement wholly by their rules is the humor of a scholar."—Francis Bacon

"Touch not; taste not; handle not." —Epistle of Paul

"Blot out vain pomp; check impulse; quench appetite; keep reason under its own control." —Marcus Aurelius

"Some were too young to have married; some, for various reasons, had left their families behind; others were young bachelors who hoped to marry as soon as they accumulated a few dollars—all of them needed a family environment that would ease their loneliness." —Cyril Ray, "Robert Mondavi of the Napa Valley"

NOTE: PATTERNS 6 and 9a combine here.

> "The men begged to be taken in; they promised they would help with the housework; they tugged mercilessly at her heart."—Cyril Ray, "Robert Mondavi of the Napa Valley"

> "Youth is not a time of life; it is a state of mind; it is not a matter of rosy cheeks, red lips and supple knees; it is a matter of will, a quality of imagination, a vigor of the emotions; it is the freshness of the deep spring of life."—Stanley Ullman, fifteenth-century French essayist

> "In their enchanted forest they built a forge and craft shops in order to earn their livings by making and selling useful and beautiful things; they built an intimate open-air theater for performances of the works of the Bard; they staged elaborate medieval pageants, in costumes of their own design, to re-create the spirit of a simpler age; in the twilight, they gathered by a bonfire to sing songs and tell stories cherishing their sense of community."—Henry Wiencek, *Smithsonian,* May 1992

Analyze below the wordiness of the preceding sentence:

_____

_____

_____

EXERCISES:

Complete each of the following sentences with a logically expressed independent clause:

1. _____ ;

the city was deserted and burning .

2. The troops bedded down early after the dawn attack ;

_____ .

3. The cat's tail began to switch back and forth ; _____

_____ .

Complete each of the following sentences by adding an appropriate conjunctive adverb:

1. The crisis had passed ; _____ we decided to

continue with our plans to leave for Spain the following week .

2. Robert would never admit that he had made a mistake ; _____

_____ he was definitely guilty of an

addition error on his income tax return .

3. Sidney was older than Grace ; _____ his knowl-

edge of world affairs was greater than hers .

In each group, combine the short sentences into one sentence that follows PATTERN 1b. If necessary, add, omit, or change words to improve the sentence.

GROUP ONE: The team looks sad.

Victory had escaped the hockey champs.

Victory does not always go to the deserving.

_____

_____

GROUP TWO: Neither Nora nor Bettie has a chance of becoming the state's gymnastic champion.

Neither wants to withdraw from the contest.

Neither wants to face the realities of failure.

_____

_____

_____

GROUP THREE: Fettucini is a delicious pasta.

It is a favorite dish in many European countries.

It is often associated with Italy.

A person who likes fettucini is not always Italian.

_____

_____

_____

As you read, watch for sentences that follow this pattern and add them below.

_____

_____

_____

_____

__ _____

_____

_____

_____

_____

PATTERN 2:	COMPOUND SENTENCE WITH

<table>
<tr><td>PATTERN 2:</td><td colspan="2">COMPOUND SENTENCE WITH
ELLIPTICAL CONSTRUCTION
(comma indicates the omitted verb)</td></tr>
<tr><td>S   V   DO or SC</td><td>; S   DO   or   SC .</td></tr>
<tr><td>(omitted verb)</td><td></td></tr>
</table>

EXPLANATION:

This pattern is really the same as PATTERN 1, but here the verb in the second clause is omitted BECAUSE and ONLY IF it would needlessly repeat the verb of the first clause. In other words, the comma says to the reader, "Here you should mentally insert the same verb you have already read in the first clause."

This construction naturally implies a need for more or less parallel wording in both clauses; the verb, of course, must be exactly the same.

For example, this is not parallel:

We   like   classical   music   ;

George   ,   punk   rock   .

The reader could not take the verb from the first clause and put it where the comma is, because "George like punk rock" is ungrammatical. BUT even if your wording is parallel, even if the omitted verb is exactly like the one in the first clause, you may still have an awkward-sounding sentence if you omit too many words or if you forget the importance of rhythm and sound.

For example, read this aloud:

Darby played a musical number by Bach; Joan, Beethoven.

This sentence sounds as if Darby played something written by three people!

Then read this aloud:

Darby played a musical number by Bach; Joan, one by Beethoven.

If you leave out more than the verb, you many need to insert a word, such as *one* here. Notice in the sentence above and in the two sentences below that it is possible to leave out more than just the verb; sometimes you may even leave out the subject *and* the verb:

An artist's instinct is intuitive, not rational; aesthetic, not pragmatic.

When to use this pattern:

This pattern is sophisticated, stylistically. It looks simple to create, but its structure presents some underlying difficulties. Nevertheless, when you want to avoid repeating the same verb in the second or third clause of a sentence, you may find this structure helpful. You will have to rely on your ear to know whether it's the right time for PATTERN 2. Does the sentence sound natural and have a rhythmical balance? Or is it awkward or unclear? If so, it's inappropriate.

EXAMPLES:

The Christian church and communism each have a goal: one is spiritual; the other, material.

A favorite theme song of Mexican outlaws is *La Cucaracha,* meaning "cockroach"; the most popular theme song among children, "Happy Birthday to You."

For many students the new math crusade of the 1950s was a disaster; for others, a godsend.

The famous last words of Kit Carson were "Adios, compadre!"; of Robert Louis Stevenson, "My head, my head!"

Because of the extent of both oceans, the Atlantic and the Pacific share the same boundaries; the Arctic Ocean is the northern; the Antarctic, the southern.

A red light means stop; a green light, go.

PROFESSIONAL EXAMPLES:

"Thought is the blossom; language [,] the bud; action [,] the fruit."— Ralph Waldo Emerson

NOTE: The brackets indicate that the commas do not appear in the original sentence.

"Washington, D.C., has 92 police officers per 10,000 people; New Jersey, 41; West Virginia, 16."—*Condé Nast Traveler,* August 1992

CHECKPOINTS:

✔ Be sure that there really are two independent clauses in the sentence even though the second one has an unexpressed verb.

✔ Be sure that the verb omitted in the second clause matches exactly, in form and tense, the verb in the first clause.

✔ Apply the following rule to whatever you omit after the semicolon: If more than the verb is left out, the structure must be parallel and the thought be complete.

✔ Use a semicolon if there is no conjunction; use a comma if there is a joining, coordinating conjunction.

EXERCISES:

Complete each of the following sentences. (1) Use a comma in the second clause to substitute for the verb in the first clause. (2) Write a complete thought for a missing first clause.

1. The green light at the end of Daisy's dock represents hope for Jay ;

_____

_____ .

2. A threatening sky with black clouds usually signals an approaching storm ; _____

_____ .

3. _____ ;

Passover and Easter, the season of renewal .

4. An owl symbolizes wisdom ; _____ .

5. All the children wanted to go to McDonald's for lunch ; _____

_____ .

As you read, watch for sentences that follow this pattern and add them below.

_____

_____

```
┌─────────────────────────────────────────────────────────────┐
│  PATTERN 3:          COMPOUND SENTENCE WITH                   │
│                      EXPLANATORY STATEMENT                    │
│                    (clauses separated by a colon)             │
│  ─────────────────────────────────────────────────────────   │
│  General statement (idea) : specific statement (example) .    │
│  ─────────────────────────   ────────────────────────────     │
│  (an independent clause)       (an independent clause)        │
└─────────────────────────────────────────────────────────────┘
```

EXPLANATION:

This pattern is exactly like PATTERNS 1 and 2 in structure: it is a compound; but it is very different in content, as the colon implies. A colon in a compound sentence performs a special function: it signals to the reader that something important or explanatory will follow (as this very sentence illustrates). In this particular pattern, the colon signals that the second clause will specifically explain or expand some idea expressed only vaguely in the first clause.

The first statement will contain a word or an idea that needs explaining; the second statement will give some specific information or example about that idea.

When to use this pattern

A whole clause receives special emphasis in this sentence. You will use it when you want the second part of a sentence to explain the first part, give an example, or provide an answer to an implied question.

As you study the following examples, notice that the first independent statement mentions something in an unspecified way: "a harsh truth," "a single horrifying meaning." Then the independent statement after the colon answers your questions: "What harsh truth?" "Which horrifying meaning?" In short, the second clause makes the first one clear.

EXAMPLES:

Darwin's *Origin of Species* forcibly states a harsh truth: only the fittest survive.

The empty coffin in the center of the crypt had a single horrifying meaning: Dracula had left his tomb to stalk the village streets in search of fresh blood.

Remember what the old saying prudently advises: Be careful what you wish for because you may actually get it.

NOTE: Some writers capitalize the first word after the colon in this pattern, but this capitalization is a matter of personal taste and styling.

A lizard never worries about losing its tail: it can always grow another.

"Not all basketball players use the same technique in shooting free throws: some of them shoot the ball from over their heads and others use the 'granny' shot, which they shoot from the waist and project upwards."—Jimmy Salem

"Weekdays are very similar to identical suitcases: they are all the same size, but some people can pack more into them than others."—Joel Gutierrez

No one, however, would deny that George Patton did what generals were primarily expected to do: he won battles.

Little Red Riding Hood lied: wolves don't eat grandmothers; they eat elk, bison, and deer.

PROFESSIONAL EXAMPLES:

"Topographically, the North and South Islands [of New Zealand] are quite different: They are separate microcontinents in collision, the more temperate North molded by volcanic fires; the cooler South by ice."—C. D. B. Bryan, *European Travel and Life,* June/July 1990

"Sociologists continue to be vexed by the pathology of urban violence: Why is it so random, so fierce, so easily triggered?"—Edward Ayers

"Look closely around your garden: you may find one of the hummingbirds' egg-cup nests—often in some precarious, fairly public spot like the top of a ripening orange or woven into foliage at the end of a redwood branch."—Jim McCausland, *Sunset Magazine*

"The *regadores* know, by consulting a list, where water should be flowing at any particular time: if their list says a certain field must get half an hour of water, they make sure that it gets half an hour, no more, no less."—Nick Inman and Clara Villanueva, *Lookout,* April 1992

"For even in the early days of smelting and working metal, the blades could certainly cut: the romances abound with descriptions of men being cut in half, from helmet to thigh, of arm and shoulder lopped off with one stroke, of two legs severed at the knee as if they were fennel stalks."—Graeme Fife, *Arthur the King*

"Old cars and young children have several things in common: Both are a responsibility and have to be fed often or they break down."— Claudia Glenn Downing, *Lear's,* November 1992

NOTE: This sentence has a capital letter after the colon and a final clause beginning with the coordinator *or.* The final clause is so short that the author chose to omit the comma before the coordinator.

CHECKPOINTS:

✔ Now that you have learned all three of the compound constructions, notice the differences among them. PATTERNS 1, 2, and 3 are NOT simply three different ways to punctuate the same sentence. The words must perform different functions; the sentences must do different things:

PATTERN 1 must make two closely related statements about the same idea, statements you do not want to punctuate as two separate sentences;

PATTERN 2 must have a specific word or words from the first clause implied in the second—otherwise no ellipsis is possible;

PATTERN 3 must have a second independent clause that in some way amplifies or explains the idea stated in the first independent clause.

✔ Do not use this pattern with a colon unless the second statement is related to the first.

✔ Remember the test for every compound sentence: both clauses must be full statements and capable of standing alone as sentences.

EXERCISES:

Complete each of the following sentences with an independent clause that (1) answers an implied question, (2) provides an example, or (3) gives further explanation:

1. _____ :

all the graduates cheered as President Arneson conferred their degrees .

2. The products of Japan represent a genuine threat to many American industries : _____

_____ .

3. At least I know one way *not* to clean out a radiator : _____

_____ .

4. The new world champion body builder told the reporters that she had to leave : _____

_____ .

5. _____ :

we toured the National Air and Space Museum, The Smithsonian Castle, the Freer Gallery, and the new wing of the National Gallery of Art .

As you read, watch for sentences that follow this pattern and add them below.

_____

_____

_____

_____

_____

_____

Sentences with series

What is a series?

When you see or hear the word *series,* what comes immediately to mind? The World Series? A bowling series? A television series? Now let's think about how the word *series* applies to sentence structure.

A series is a group of three or more similar items, all of which go in the same slot of the sentence. All items in the series must be similar in form (for example, all nouns or all verbs) because they have the same grammatical function. You may have a series in any slot of the sentence: three or four verbs for the same subject; three or four objects for the same preposition; three or four nouns or adjectives in the object or complement slot. You may have a series with any part of speech, not only with single words but also with phrases or dependent clauses. You may also arrange the items in different patterns:

A , B , C   A and B and C   A , B , and C

or with paired items:

A and B   C and D   E and F

When is a series helpful?

A series is a good way to eliminate wordiness. If, for example, you have three short sentences, you may be able to reduce them to a single sentence with a series somewhere in it. If you are listing or giving several examples, try series structures to provide details. For variety, you might create this pattern without the conjunction, thereby giving a different kind of emphasis to the items of the series. You are not singling out the last item for special emphasis; instead, you're saying that all of the items are equal.

PATTERN 4: A SERIES WITHOUT A CONJUNCTION
(a series in any part of the sentence)

A , B , C _____ .

EXPLANATION:

This pattern is the simplest form of the series. The items are separated by commas, and in this special pattern no conjunction links the final two items. Omitting this conjunction is effective, for it gives your sentence a quick, staccato sound.

Develop your ear!

Read the series aloud so that you hear whether the items flow together smoothly and euphoniously *without* the conjunction before the last item. Remember that tone and sound and fluency are important considerations here. Also, remember that each item should receive equal emphasis. None is more important than the others.

EXAMPLES:

The coach is loud, profane, demonstrative; he has again been trapped, caught, humiliated.

With wisdom, patience, virtue, Queen Victoria directed the course of nineteenth-century England.

The United States has a government of the people, by the people, for the people.

Since unification in Berlin, walls have come down, barriers have been broken, bonds have been formed.

Big burgers with everything on 'em: pickles, onions, tomato, lettuce, plenty of mustard.

(Note the fragment.)

PROFESSIONAL EXAMPLES:

"And [the film star] looks every inch the actor: painted, powdered, affected, vain, insecure, unreal, quite frightening, grotesque."— Dundan Fallowell, *European Travel and Life,* September 1990

"Our priorities run to safety over style, value over flash, comfort over speed."—Caroline Miller, *Lear,* April 1993

"Oil booms are short-lived, speculative, ruinous to those who rely on them."—Paul Burka, *Texas Monthly*

"Whether 60 or 16, there is in every human being's heart the love of wonder, the sweet amazement of the stars and the starlike things, the undaunted challenge of events, the unfailing childlike appetite of 'what-next' in the joy of the game of living."—Stanley Ullman, fifteenth-century French essayist

"Respectable New Mexico historians lament the public's obsession with Billy the Kid. They prefer to highlight the genuine builders of the ancient land of scenic beauty and cultural diversity—Coronado, Onate, De Vargas, Stephen Watts Kearney, Kit Carson, Manuelito, Victorio, Archbishop Lamy, the Oteros, Georgia O'Keeffe."

"Guerin sat high on the concrete bank at freeway side, staring idly down upon the river of traffic beneath him: automobiles, taxis, panel trucks, dunebuggies with whiplash antennae, besurfboarded woodies, 24- and 32-wheeled big irons, groaning beer trucks and cement mixers, even an occasional police cruiser or wailing ambulance rolled below . . . ."—Les Standiford, "Guerin and the Sail Cat Blues"

SENTENCES FOR ANALYSIS:

Look carefully at the following series patterns. Do you get lost as you read them? Is there too much detail?

1. Do you see ways of breaking up this overlong sentence into two or more shorter ones that are not overwhelming? Or do you think the sentence is effective stylistically?

"Robert Mondavi's father, Cesare, came from Sassafarento near Ancona, on the Adriatic coast of the Marches—not a particularly rich or fertile part of Italy even now, nor, except for Verdicchio, much of a wine-growing region, and a good deal less so, no doubt, in 1883, when Cesare was born, the son of a large, simple family and possibly the first member of it, I have read somewhere, to be able to sign his name."—Cyril Ray, "Robert Mondavi of the Napa Valley."

2. The following sentence has a lengthy series joined by repeated possessive pronouns. Do you think the sentence is effective or weak? What feature contributes strength or detracts from the rhetorical effectiveness?

"Walled off from the roaring traffic of the Embankment and Fleet Street and High Holborn, each Inn is a self-centered community with its own gardens, lush with cherry and magnolia, camelia, and crocus; its own library; its own dining hall; its labyrinth of walks and lawns; its blocks of offices and flats let out mostly to barristers."—Robert Wernick, *Smithsonian,* May 1992

3. Watch how Kathryn Marshall combines a number of rhetorical strategies with her series structures. She alludes to Bugsy Segal and the founding of Las Vegas, she underscores her emotion by repeating the word *ever,* and she creates a number of images with her various verb choices suggesting the movement of light.

"In my room, I stood at the darkened window and looked out at the neo-wonderland. The lights rippled, rolled, darted, sequenced their way through fantastical patterns against the black, empty screen of beyond, millions and millions of lights, more than crazy Bugsy could have imagined, far more than someone who's never spent a night in Las Vegas could ever, ever, ever—even in the wildest reaches of dreams—hope to comprehend."—Kathryn Marshall, *American Way,* September 1991

CHECKPOINT:

✔ Since any part of the sentence may have a series, take care to make all items in the series parallel in form as they are already parallel in function.

Find the items that are not parallel in these awkward sentences:

The typical teenage user of snuff is white, active, and athletic, and subjected to very heavy peer pressure.

Swimming, surfing, to go boating—these were Sally's favorite sports at the summer camp.

Now explain why these revisions are better:

The typical teenage user of snuff is white, active, athletic, and peer pressure is very heavy.

Swimming, surfing, boating—these were Sally's favorite sports at the summer camp.

NOTE: Although the commonest pattern for series—A, B, and C—is not discussed in this book, you should remember that a comma before the conjunction helps to make the meaning clear.

> Shakespeare uses an image, a metaphor, a simile and rhyme scheme to clarify his theme in this sonnet. (A "simile and rhyme" scheme? Without the comma before the conjunction, that's what the sentence says!)

> The restaurant served four varieties of sandwiches: corned beef, pastrami, salami and egg with bacon. (Would you order the last one?)

NOTE: Some style manuals, such as those for journalists and technical writers in the military, omit the comma before the conjunction and the last item.

EXERCISES:

Develop a series for each of the following sentences.

1. A theme traditionally has three major parts :

_____ , _____ ,

_____

2. _____ , _____ ,

_____ are my favorite summertime activities .

3. (Begin this sentence with three -*ed* or -*en* words.)

_____ , _____

_____ , _____ , the gambler stag-

gered away from the poker table with only a few coins in change .

4. (Provide a series of -*ing* words for the blanks.) The players

formed a wide circle around the coach , _____ ,

_____ , _____ ,

_____ .

5. After the announcement on the loudspeaker the rowdy spectators

at the tennis match _____ ,

_____ , _____

As you read, watch for sentences that follow this pattern and add them
below.

_____

_____

_____

_____

_____

_____

_____

```
┌────────────────────────────────────────────────────────────────┐
│  PATTERN 4a:          A SERIES WITH A VARIATION                  │
│                                                                  │
│  A or B or C        .      (in any place in the sentence)        │
│  A and B and C      .      (in any place in the sentence)        │
└────────────────────────────────────────────────────────────────┘
```

EXPLANATION:

Occasionally, you will want to vary the preceding pattern and instead write a series with conjunctions between all items (but usually not more than three). Again, let your ear be your guide. Listen for the tumbling rhythm in the following sentences.

EXAMPLES:

Peering down from the hill, Merlin could see the castle swathed in gloom and fear and death.

Despite his handicaps, I have never seen Larry angry or cross or depressed.

Many ice hockey games lead to broken ribs or sprained knees or dislocated shoulders—or even worse.

Collies and geese and children tumbled out of the farmhouses in Alsace Lorraine, barking or hissing or shouting according to their unique French natures.

The intense heat and the exhaustion and the twenty-six miles had confused and crippled Gabriela Scheiss, but there was something in her spirit that sustained her during the 1988 Los Angeles Olympic marathon.

PROFESSIONAL EXAMPLES:

"During World War II from fall into the summer of 1940, Germany rolled into Poland and Denmark and Norway and Holland and Belgium and finally France."—Fred Strebeigh, *Smithsonian*

(Do you think a dash before the final *and* would have made the sentence more dramatic?)

"This gentle physician, without the support of the media, or demagogues, or throngs of intimidating supporters, or whites from

New England, or large sums of shame money, or religious back-ing, quietly and with dignity took his case to the United States Supreme Court with an El Paso attorney unlicensed to practice before that tribunal."—Leon Metz, "On Books," *El Paso Herald-Post,* September 25, 1992

(Note that this author uses a comma after each item in the series.)

SENTENCES FOR ANALYSIS:

Not all writers are fully in control of their style. Often you'll find in your reading long sentences piled so full of information that you lose the train of the author's thought.

1. Note how Clark Kimball overloads the sentence below with printing vocabulary. Since Kimball is lecturing, is this long sentence more—or less—of a problem than if he were writing? Is the sentence suc-cessful, or do you have trouble remembering earlier parts by the time you reach the end? How might you break up the sentence into two or three shorter ones?

"The paper, the ink, the letter forms—the Romans, the italics, the serifs and sans serifs—the ligatures, impressions, spacing, leading, margin, gutter; the plates, illustrations, frontispieces, head and tail pieces; colophons; borders, rules, folios, ding-bats; title pages, half-titles; cloths, papers, boards; stampings, debossings, labels, bands, cases—these are some of the words of the typographer—challenging and magic words—each laden and potent with meaning—each of which must be put at the service of the subject matter, and simulta-neously in harmony with each other!"—Clark Kimball, Carl Hertzog Lecture Series, *The Southwest Printer,* 1990

---

2. Analyze the following sentence for its length, detail, punctuation, and clarity: "Sir Thomas More and Sir Francis Drake and Sir Walter Raleigh and Shakespeare's Sir John Falstaff, Sir Francis Bacon and John Donne, Sir William Blackstone and William Penn and William Pitt, Boswell and Fielding and Sheridan and De Quincy and Lamb and Thackeray and Macaulay, King Edward VII, Margaret Thatcher, and of course, Rumpole of the Bailey—all took their meals at an Inn of Court."—Henry Wiencek, *Smithsonian,* May 1992

---

3. Here is another series that loses readers. How could you eliminate some of the clumsiness? What makes the sentence so forbidding?

"The Prado offers as breathtaking a panorama of soaring peaks like Velazquez and Francisco Goya and Hieronymus Bosch and El Greco and Titian and Bartolome Esteban Murillo and Jose Ribera and Peter Paul Rubens and Sandro Botticelli, with stretches of flatland or desert in between."—Stanley Meisler, "Spain's Prado," *Smithsonian,* January 1992

EXERCISES:

For each of the following incomplete sentences create a series with conjunctions, omitting commas.

1. Looking toward Mount Franklin, I could see that the fading afternoon sun had tinted it _____

and _____ and _____

_____ .

2. In order to win the television ratings war I suggest NBC drop

_____ and _____

_____ and _____

3. _____ and _____

_____ and _____ seem

to be the issues in the presidential campaign .

4. The professor asked the class: "What will be the predominant source of energy in the next decade: _____

_____ or _____ or

_____ ?"

5. All that is _____ or _____

_____or _____ or

_____ seems to be harmful to one's health .

Write sentences using the series listed below. For one group use no conjunctions between the items; in another add a conjunction between them.

1. spaghetti   vermicelli   ravioli   macaroni

_____

_____

_____

2. soccer in spring   baseball in summer
   hockey in winter   football in the fall

_____

_____

_____

3. baked potatoes   boiled potatoes   mashed potatoes

_____

_____

_____

As you read, watch for sentences that follow this pattern and add them below.

_____

_____

_____

_____

_____

_____

_____

_____

_____

<table>
<tr><td>PATTERN 5:</td><td>A SERIES OF BALANCED PAIRS
(note the rhythm)</td></tr>
</table>

A and B   ,   C and D   ,   E and F   .

(may be in any slot in the sentence)

EXPLANATION:

This pattern has a series with an *even* number of items—four or six or eight. Balance these in pairs with a conjunction between the items in each pair. This construction creates a balanced rhythm, but is this rhythm right for your sentence? Read the sentence aloud; listen to the cadence of your words because *rhythm* is the important feature. Does your sentence have an orderly progression with a kind of climactic order? Can you hear the items balanced against each other? Do you like the way the paired words sound together?

NOTE: There are other coordinating conjunctions besides *and* and *or.* See the fourth example below.

EXAMPLES:

The actual herbs in special vinegars—thyme and basil, rosemary and garlic, hot pepper and chive—float in beautifully designed bottles.

The story of Spain is a history of kings and poets, saints and conquistadores, emperors and revolutionaries, Cervantes and Picasso, Franco and Juan Carlos, the Alhambra and the Escorial.

Antony and Cleopatra, Romeo and Juliet, Tristan and Isolde, Lancelot and Guinevere were all famous lovers in literature.

Eager yet fearful, confident but somewhat suspicious, Jason eyed the barber who would give him his first haircut.

(This is a variation of the pattern.)

The author knew the distinctions that existed between liberals and conservatives, between vampires and vixens, between swashbucklers and the timid, between the exploited and the victimized.

PROFESSIONAL EXAMPLES:

"Before Uriah Heep I have step by step abandoned name and reputation, peace and quiet, house and home."— Charles Dickens, *David Copperfield*

Germany, which "produced Adolph Hitler and Ludwig van Beethoven, Karl Marx and Albert Einstein, poison gas and the BMW, World War II and the first X-ray machine, will soon be, once more, the leading power in Europe."—Fergus Bordewich, *Reader's Digest,* December 1990

"It's amazing how lifeless elements like stone and wood, nails and plaster, glass and metal take on a soul after you turn them into a house."—Jane Porcino, *Modern Maturity,* April 1993

"God is day and night, winter and summer, war and peace, surfeit and hunger."—Heraclitus

"It's a story of money and power, passion and obsession, ambition and greed, love and hate, good and evil, temptation and frenzy of a dangerous yet erotic game, brought keenly alive, and set against the panorama of brilliant riches of energy and real estate during euphoric boom times in the Sunbelt."—Louis Bodnar, reviewing *Sunbelt* in the *El Paso Herald-Post*

"No man is really happy or safe without a hobby, and it makes precious little difference what the outside interest may be—botany, beetles, or butterflies; roses, tulips, or irises; fishing, mountaineering, or antiques—anything will do so long as he straddles a hobby and rides it hard."—Sir William Osler

NOTE: This sentence is a variation on a balanced series. Semicolons join the items of the series, which have internal punctuation.

"Drawing on newspapers and other published accounts from the period, Penick lets those most affected—male and female, educated and ignorant, preachers and sinners, scientists, rivermen, merchants, Indians and an undifferentiated assortment—describe their brush with one of nature's fiercest forces."

NOTE: This sentence, from a review of James Penick's *The New Madrid Earthquakes of 1811–1812,* combines PATTERNS 5, 11, and 12. Can you find other patterns as well?

EXERCISES:

Complete each of the following sentences. Fill the blanks with a series of balanced pairs.

1. Martini or daiquiri , _____ or

_____ , _____

or _____ — these are popular drinks .

2. If you are making up a list of popular comedians from film
or television, you might want to consider my favorites :
_____ and _____

_____ , _____ and _____

_____ , _____ and _____

_____ .

3. Americans choose both a president and a vice president every four
years; in the past we have chosen from _____

_____ and _____

_____ , _____ and

_____ and _____ .

4. Comic strip husbands and wives like _____

_____ and _____

or _____ and _____

_____ provide _____ .

Using the words listed below, compose three sentences, each with a
balanced series pattern:

1. ham   eggs   coffee   fruit   toast   jam

_____

_____

2. lions   tigers   leopards   cheetahs

_____

_____

3. Halloween   Thanksgiving   Christmas   New Year's Eve

_____

_____

As you read, watch for sentences that follow this pattern and add them below.

_____

_____

_____

_____

_____

_____

_____

_____

**AN INTRODUCTORY SERIES
OF APPOSITIVES**
(with a dash and a summarizing subject)

Appositive , appositive , appositive — summary word S V .
....

(The key summarizing word before the subject may be one of these: *such, all, those, this, many, each, which, what, these, something, someone.* Sometimes this summary word will be the subject, but other times it will merely modify the subject.)

EXPLANATION:

This pattern begins with a "cluster" of appositives. An appositive is simply another word for something named elsewhere in the sentence— that is, it is another name for some noun. The appositives are followed, in sequence, by a dash, a word that summarizes the appositives, and the subject—verb combination for the main clause. You may arrange the appositives in any of the patterns for series (see PATTERNS 4, 4a, and 5).

PATTERN 6 produces a highly stylized sentence that is extremely effective for special places in your writing, places where you want to squeeze a lot of information into the same slot.

EXAMPLES:

The petty, the wronged, the fallen, the cowardly, the righteous, the deluded, the rapacious, the unctuous—each played a role on the stage of Cervantes' vast human drama.

Vanity, greed, corruption—which serves as the novel's source of conflict?

The crack of the lion trainer's whip, the dissonant music of the calliope, the neighs of Arabian stallions—such sounds mean "circus" to all children.

Chinese and Indians, Malays, Thais, Koreans, Vietnamese—all of these ethnic groups vie for your attention in Singapore.

Disko kloobs, verd processer, ti-shirti, konsulting, gala-konsert—these are some of the *Amerikanizatsia* of current Russian.

Bull riding, camel races, bronc riding, and roping—these events mean "rodeo" to many people; they mean money to the cowboys.

(This example combines PATTERNS 1 and 6.)

The *Mona Lisa*, Michaelangelo's *David,* the frescoes in the Sistine Chapel—what an imagination those Italians had!

OR: —which of these is the best proof of the Italian imagination?

OR: —many are the wonders of the Renaissance in Italy.

An old photograph, a haunting fragrance, a sudden view of a half-forgotten scene—something unexpectedly triggers our nostalgia for the past.

NOTE: Sometimes these appositives come at the end. Try reversing any of the sentences above, following the example below:

The tea tax, the lack of representation, the distance from the mother country, the growing sense of being a new and independent nation—what do you think caused the American Revolution?

What do you think caused the American Revolution—the tea tax, the lack of representation, the distance from the mother country, or the growing sense of being a new and independent nation?

PROFESSIONAL EXAMPLES:

"Worry, doubt, self-disgust, fear, and despair—these bow the head and turn the spirit back to dust."—Stanley Ullman, fifteenth-century essayist

"Shipwrecks, drownings, mutinies, scurvy, starvation—all were part of every Renaissance mariner's life."—"Columbus," *American Heritage*

CHECKPOINTS:

✔ Check the punctuation of this pattern:

1. there must be commas between the appositives in the series;

2. there must be a dash after the series.

✔ Check that there is a summary word at the beginning of the main clause.

✔ Check that, as in any series, all the appositives are parallel in structure and related in meaning.

EXERCISES:

For each sentence supply introductory appositives that logically attach to the independent clause.

1. _____ , _____ ,

_____ — each of these people served their

country well .

2. To _____ , to _____ ,

to _____ — such are the goals of the average

American college graduate .

3. _____ or _____ ,

_____ or _____ ,

_____ or _____ —

what are your preferences for spring break ?

Complete each sentence by writing an appropriate summarizing word and independent clause.

1. Acceptance , happiness , success — _____

_____

_____ .

2. Poetry and music , painting and sculpture , drama and dance — ___

_____

_____ .

As you read, watch for sentences that follow this pattern and add them below.

_____

_____

_____

_____

_____

_____

_____

_____

```
┌─────────────────────────────────────────────────────────────────┐
│                                                                   │
│  PATTERN 7:          AN INTERNAL SERIES OF                        │
│                      APPOSITIVES OR MODIFIERS                     │
│                      (enclosed by a pair of dashes or parentheses)│
│                                                                   │
│                    ―――                                      ―――    │
│        S    OR     appositive , appositive , appositive    OR   V │
│             (        modifier , modifier , modifier     )         │
│                                                                   │
└─────────────────────────────────────────────────────────────────┘
```

EXPLANATION:

The beginning of the sentence (or the end) is not the only place where you may have a series of appositives or modifiers. Appositives will rename and modifiers will describe something named elsewhere in the sentence. Any kind of series (see PATTERNS 4, 4a, and 5) may come between the subject and the verb, between two subjects, and so on. Because this kind of series is a dramatic interruption within the sentence and may even have commas between the items, there *must* be a dash before and a dash after it.

But when would you select parentheses to enclose the appositives or modifiers? Parentheses set off information that is less important or could even be omitted. It's as if you have your hand up to your lips to conceal what you're saying or to direct your message to a special audience. Think of an actor on stage whispering something to another character or to the audience in an aside (that is, conveying information not meant for everyone to hear).

A modifier, unlike an appositive, is not a substitute for another word. Modifiers describe and give additional information about a single word or even a whole sentence. Although both modifiers and appositives are movable, a modifier must follow closely the word group it describes. If you place a modifier incorrectly, you may confuse your reader with a "dangling" construction (see PATTERN 12).

EXAMPLES:

                    DO
The necessary qualities for political life—guile, ruthlessness, and
                    S   V
        garrulity—he learned by carefully studying his father's life.

(This example illustrates a variation of the pattern, in which the direct object precedes the subject—verb.)

My favorite red wines—Zinfandel, Cabernet Sauvignon, Pinot Noir—
blend well in making California rosé wines.

The basic fencing moves (the advance, the retreat, the lunge) demand
careful balance by both fencers.

(Try using dashes instead of parentheses in this sentence. What subtle
changes in meaning are suggested by the different punctuation choices?)

Dozens of charmingly decorated *casetas*—bright red with an occasional purple door or plain white with banners and religious icons
over the door—spring up along Calle Juan Carlos.

Many of the books kids enjoy reading *(Little Women, Jane Eyre, David
Copperfield)* portray women in traditional and often uncompli-
mentary roles.

The much despised predators—mountain lions, timber wolves, and
grizzly bears—have been shot, trapped, and poisoned so relent-
lessly for so long that they have nearly vanished from their old
haunts.

PROFESSIONAL EXAMPLE:

"When the matador takes the sword and muleta and advances toward
his adversary, the public—aristocratic bull breeders in English
tweeds, movie stars and politicians, wealthy fans from Latin
America—is suddenly hushed; the 'silence of Seville,' the sound
of twelve thousand people being absolutely quiet, are unique,
almost fearsome."—William Lyon, "Lord of the Ring,"
Connoisseur, October 1991

CHECKPOINTS:

✔ Do you have two dashes or a pair of parentheses? TWO such
marks, not one, are required to set off a pair.

✔ Can you read a "complete sentence" even after you eliminate the
interrupting appositives or modifiers? In other words, does the sentence convey its message without the words between the dashes? If so,
you have punctuated properly, for the function of the dashes or parentheses is to indicate an interrupter that could be omitted.

EXERCISES:

Add an internal series of modifiers or appositives to complete each of the following sentences:

1. Which famous television personality — _____

_____ or _____

or _____ — do you think will win this year's

Emmy Award ?

2. The youthful knight — _____ ,

_____ , and _____

— entered the jousting contest to impress the princess he hoped to

marry .

3. Television commercials — _____ and

_____ , and _____

—hammer ruthlessly on the viewer's mind .

Complete each of the following sentences by incorporating the internal appositives or modifiers as suggested.

1. _____ — sociology or psychology or eco-

nomics or political science — _____ .

2. _____ — coordination , agility , speed —

_____ .

3. _____ — lasagna and ravioli ,

spaghetti and meatballs , spumoni and tortoni — _____

_____ .

4. _____ — perfumed body , seductive smile ,

suntanned legs — _____ .

As you read, watch for sentences that follow this pattern and add them below.

_____

_____

_____

_____

_____

_____

_____

_____

_____

| PATTERN 7a: | A VARIATION: A SINGLE APPOSITIVE OR A PAIR |

```
                    OR          OR
                    __          __
_____S_____    (     appositive    )  _____V_____
                    OR          OR
                    ,           ,
```

(Use two dashes or parentheses or commas to enclose this appositive.)

EXPLANATION:

This pattern resembles PATTERN 7 except that it has only one or two items for the appositive instead of a full series. Here, the appositive may or may not have modifiers. In this variation, there is also an interruption in thought immediately after the subject, but the appositive can have a variety of effects, depending on your punctuation:

   a. a pair of dashes will make the appositive dramatic;

   b. parentheses will make it almost whisper;

   c. a pair of commas will make it nearly inconspicuous because they are so ordinary.

EXAMPLES:

A sudden explosion—artillery fire—signaled the beginning of a barrage.

A familiar smell—fresh blood—assailed his jungle-trained nostrils.

My current plan, to change my major from marketing to civil engineering, is on hold for the moment.

(Here an infinitive acts as a modifier of the subject and interrupts the subject—verb combination.)

A popular theory among climatologists (the greenhouse effect) suggests how the earth's changing temperature threatens humanity.

His former wife (once a famous Philadelphia model) now owns a well-known boutique in the Bahamas.

The slogan of the firm—"See Texas First"—helped promote tourism.

The first man to walk on the moon, Neil Alden Armstrong, is a man whom the world will never forget.

PROFESSIONAL EXAMPLE:

"But the show's most famous motto—"Live long and prosper!"—proved to be downright prophetic."—Michael Logan, *TV Guide.*

CHECKPOINT:

✔ Again, remember that TWO, not one, are needed to make a pair—two dashes, a pair of parentheses, two commas.

EXERCISES:

Provide a missing appositive or pair of appositives or supply other words to complete each sentence:

1. The familiar cheer of the football team — _____

_____ — began to appear on bumper

stickers around the town .

2. _____ (my wife and best friend)

_____

_____ .

3. Those two bright colors — _____ and

_____ — are prominent in all of the artist's later

paintings .

4. Two ancient skills of the artists — _____

and _____ — can never be successfully imitated

by contemporary craftsmen .

5. _____ (filing for bankruptcy) shocked

the members of the country club .

Make up an original sentence using each of the following words as an interrupting appositive:

1. Christopher Columbus _____

_____

2. pineapple juice _____

_____

3. her allowance _____

_____

As you read, watch for sentences that follow this pattern and add them below.

_____

_____

_____

_____

_____

_____

_____

_____

PATTERN 8:   DEPENDENT CLAUSES IN A PAIR
                OR IN A SERIES
              (at beginning or end of sentence)

If . . . , if . . . , if . . . , ___then___ S   V .

When . . . , when . . . , when . . . , S   V

S   V   that . . . , that . . . , that . . .   .

(omit the third clause and have just two, if you wish)

EXPLANATION:

The preceding patterns have shown series with single words or phrases. PATTERN 8 shows a series with dependent clauses. All of the clauses in this series must be dependent; they must also be parallel in structure; they must express conditions or situations or provisions dependent upon the idea expressed in the main clause. The series may come at the beginning or at the end of the sentence. You will normally have two or three clauses here; rarely will four or five sound graceful and smooth. Try not to struggle for style; be natural, relaxed, never forced.

This pattern is unique. Save it for special places, special functions. It is particularly helpful

a. at the end of a single paragraph to summarize the major points;

b. in structuring a thesis statement having three or more parts (or points);

c. in the introductory or concluding paragraph to bring together the main points of a composition in a single sentence.

EXAMPLES:

Because it may seem difficult at first, because it may sound awkward or forced, because it often creates lengthy sentences where the thought "gets lost," this pattern seems forbidding to some writers, but it isn't all that hard; try it.

When he smelled the pungent odor of pine, when he heard the chatter of jays interrupting the silence, when he saw the startled doe, the hunter knew he had reached the center of the forest.

48

Whether one needs fantasy or whether one needs stark realism, the theater can become a mirror of life.

Since he had little imagination and since he displayed even less talent, he wasn't hired for the job.

Alison was convinced that her point of view was the right one, that she was entitled to act on it, and that ultimately her parents would approve.

PROFESSIONAL EXAMPLES:

"If radio's slim fingers can pluck music out of the night and toss it over mountains and sea; if the petal-white notes from a violin are blown across the desert and the city's din; if songs, like crimson roses, are caught from this blue air—why should mortals wonder if God hears prayer?"—Marvin Drake, *Catholic Digest*

"If your clothes are made of cotton or wool, if you wash them with soap instead of detergent, and if you hang them on the line to dry, you may not need a fabric softener."—*Consumer Reports,* February 1991

"Yet, when we do something monumental, when we establish policy that shakes the continent, when we overturn an unjust system, instead of feeling good all over and shouting the accomplishment to the heavens, we bury it on the back page or flash it on the Sunday TV news at 5:50 p.m."—Leon Metz, "On Books," *El Paso Herald-Post,* September 25, 1992

"I think of a city without cars, where dogs can dawdle, snuffing the wind; where everyone knows everyone else; where lions have wings; where cats and pigeons ignore one another; where people grow accustomed to living in a kind of sphere of absolute beauty, as if all of this were natural, whereas there is nothing at all natural about Venice."—Frederic Vitoux, "Life in Venice," *Travel and Life*

NOTE: This sentence combines PATTERNS 8 and 9a.

"He has achieved success who has lived well, laughed often, and loved much; who has enjoyed the trust of pure women, the respect of intelligent men, and the love of little children; who has filled his niche and accomplished his task; who has left the world a better place than he found it, whether an improved poppy, a perfect poem, or a rescued soul; who has always looked for the best in others and given them the best he had; whose life was an inspiration; whose memory a benediction."—Bessie Anderson Stanley's definition of "success" in *Brown Book Magazine,* 1904, as quoted in "Dear Abby," July 1992

NOTE: Here the dependent clauses with internal punctuation are joined by semicolons.

SENTENCE FOR ANALYSIS:

Do you think this sentence is effective stylistically? Does the tone complement the content?

"I wish I could say that I discovered Arden in some appropriately romantic fashion—that my Land Rover was stopped by hooded archers in a bosky byway; that I was kidnapped by free-love agitators on a dark and stormy night; or that I tracked a fugitive Soviet coup meister to a secret Stalinist camp in the Delaware woods."—Henry Wiencek, *Smithsonian,* May 1992

_____

_____

CHECKPOINTS:

✔ Don't think there must always be three dependent clauses here. Two will work in this pattern also.

✔ Whether you have only two or a full series of three or more, whether you have the clauses at the beginning or the end of the sentence, arrange them in some order of increasing impact.

EXERCISES:

Fill in the blanks to construct logical dependent or independent clauses.

1. If your mother tells you to be home by nine, it
_____ , or if _____ , you'd better
follow your mother's wishes rather than your sister's or your
friend's .

2. When _____ ,

when the astronaut heard the explosion, when the air controller

_____ , then the flight crew

_____ .

3. The landlord _____

because _____

and because _____ .

4. Whether you think _____

or whether you think _____ , you

_____ .

5. The basketball coach shouted that the referee _____

_____ , that the other team's coach

_____ , and that

_____

As you read, watch for sentences that follow this pattern and add them
below.

_____

_____

_____

_____

_____

_____

_____

Repetitions

What are repetitions?

A repetition is a restatement of a term; you may repeat the term once or several times within a sentence or a paragraph.

Why use repetitions?

Repetitions help to echo key words, to emphasize important ideas or main points, to unify sentences, or to develop coherence among sentences. Skillful repetitions of important words or phrases create "echoes" in the reader's mind: they emphasize and point out key ideas. Sometimes you will use these "echo words" in different sentences— even in different paragraphs—to help "hook" your ideas together. Be careful, though, to avoid meaningless repetition that suggests mental laziness or an inadequate vocabulary.

How do you create repetitions?

Simply allow some important word to recur in a sentence or in a paragraph or even in different paragraphs. These "echo words" may come any place in the sentence: with the subjects or the verbs, with the objects or the complements, with prepositions or other parts of speech. You need not always repeat the word exactly; think of other forms the word may take, such as *freak* (noun), *freakiness* (noun), *freakishness* (noun), *freaking* (participle), *freaky* (adjective), *freakish* (adjective), and *freakishly* and *freakily* (adverbs).

Where is repetition appropriate?

Repetition is appropriate:

    a. in different positions in the same sentence (PATTERN 9);

    b. in the same position (or "slot") of the sentence: for example, the same preposition is repeated in a series or the same word is used as object of different prepositions (PATTERN 9a).

NOTE: Once you have mastered repetitions in the same sentence, you will be ready to repeat some key words or phrases throughout your paragraphs, even from one paragraph to the next. In your reading, look for the many ways that writers effectively repeat some of their key words, placing them in strategic positions in the sentence and throughout the same paragraph. In one paragraph Rachel Carson used *sea* ten times; throughout one dramatic speech

Winston Churchill repeated the sentence "We shall fight" eight times, using it to emphasize various points.

How does punctuation affect your message?

Commas, dashes, periods, colons, and semicolons signal varying degrees of pause. A comma marks a brief pause, whereas a dash signals a longer one. There is a ring of finality in the pauses created by the colon, the semicolon, and the period. The colon suggests that important words will follow, whereas the semicolon (like the period) is an arresting mark of punctuation signaling a full stop before another idea begins.

You have probably noticed that, in all explanations (including the graphic displays that introduce each pattern), spacing before and after punctuation marks has been deliberately exaggerated so that you will pay attention to the important punctuation. When you imitate each pattern, however, you will want to use traditional spacing before and after punctuation. This spacing appears in all example sentences. If you are typing your papers, or using a word processor, remember to space twice after the **colon** (:) and to use two hyphens to distinguish a **dash** (—) from a **hyphen** (-). (See also "Why Punctuate," page 162.)

When choosing between a comma and a dash, use this guideline to determine the type of pause you need: a **comma** signals a very brief pause (it's as though you have hiccupped right in the middle of your thought); a **dash** makes you take a longer breath. A **period, colon, question mark,** or **exclamation point** requires you to pause, take a deep breath, then allows you to continue.

Consider these differences; decide what kind of pause you need; then punctuate, remembering that the various marks are not interchangeable. Each one suggests a different kind of pause.

NOTE: In each of the following three sentences, how does the punctuation change the impact and tone of the message?

> Homer, if there was a single "Homer," probably never "wrote" a word of the *Iliad.*
>
> Homer (if there was a single "Homer") probably never "wrote" a word of the *Iliad.*
>
> Homer—if there was a single "Homer"—probably never "wrote" a word of the *Iliad.*

```
┌─────────────────────────────────────────────────────────────┐
│                                                               │
│  PATTERN 9:          REPETITION OF A KEY TERM                 │
│                                                               │
│                                      ─                        │
│     S    V      key term        OR      repeated key term  .  │
│    ─────────────────────        ────   ......................  │
│                                                               │
│                                  ,                            │
│           (use dash or comma before repetition)               │
│                                                               │
└─────────────────────────────────────────────────────────────┘
```

EXPLANATION:

In this pattern you will repeat a key word in a modifying phrase attached to the main clause. You may repeat the word exactly as it is, or you may use another form of it: *brute* may become *brutal; breath* may become *breathtaking; battle* may become *battling.*

A key term is a word important enough to be repeated. It can come anywhere in the sentence, but the repetition is most common toward the end. Or, if you have a key word in the subject slot, the repetition may be, for example, a part of an interrupting modifier.

You may also vary this pattern slightly by using a dash instead of a comma; remember that the dash suggests a longer pause, a greater break in thought than the comma permits.

NOTE 1: Be sure that the word is worthy of repetition. Notice how ineffective the following "little Lulu" sentence is, and all because of the repetition of an uninteresting, overworked word:

> He was a good father, providing a good home for his good children.

NOTE 2: Be sure that the attached phrase with the repeated key term is NOT a complete sentence; if it is, you will inadvertently create a comma splice, as here:

> He was a cruel brute of a man, he was brutal to his family and even more brutal to his friends.

Here's one way of correcting the comma splice:

> He was a cruel brute of a man, brutal to his family and even more brutal to his friends.

EXAMPLES:

We all inhabit a mysterious world—the inner world, the world of the mind.

A. E. Housman used this PATTERN 9 at the end of a famous lecture: "The tree of knowledge will remain forever, as it was in the beginning, a tree to be desired to make one wise."

In "The Lottery" Shirley Jackson mocks community worship of outworn customs, customs that no longer have meaning, customs that deny man his inherent dignity and link him with the uncivilized world of beasts.

Neither the warning in the tarot cards—an ominous warning about the dangers of air flight—nor the one on her ouija board could deter Marsha from volunteering for the first Mars shot.

Looking into the cottage, we saw great splotches of blood smeared on the walls, walls that only that morning had rung with shouts of joy and merriment.

PROFESSIONAL EXAMPLES:

"Privacy, of course, has the advantage of, well, privacy."—Susin Shapiro, *Lear's,* April 1993

"Never give in, never give in, never, never, never, never—in nothing great or small, large or petty—never give in except to convictions of honor and good sense."—Winston Churchill, Address at Harrow School, October 1941

"Victory at all costs, victory in spite of all terror, victory however long and hard the road may be; for without victory there is no survival."—Winston Churchill, House of Commons, May 1940

CHECKPOINTS:

✔✔ Double check! Notice that the repetition is in a phrase, not a clause. In this pattern, the words following the dash or comma MUST NOT have a subject or a verb with the repeated word; the result would be a comma splice (comma fault).

WRONG: He was part of the older generation, his generation was born before the Depression. (This compound must have a semicolon.)

CORRECT: He was part of the older generation, a generation born before the Depression.

A frequent error occurs when there is a period or semicolon where the comma should be, thereby creating a fragment out of the modifier containing the repeated key term.

WRONG: He praises the beauty of his love. A love that is unfortunately hopeless because it is not mutual.

NOTE: This example contains the "pattern" of a very common fragment error:

<u>   S   V   </u> .   S + [dep. clause] but NO verb .

CORRECT: He praises the beauty of his love, a love unfortunately hopeless because it is not mutual.

EXERCISES:

Complete each of the following sentences by repeating the underlined word.

1. The destruction caused by the tornado was <u>devastating</u>, devastating

to _____ ,

devastating also to _____

_____ .

2. <u>Ruthless</u>—ruthless to _____

_____ , ruthless to _____

_____ — the leader of the insurgents showed

no mercy to the unlucky civilians who lived in the community .

3. The faithful worshipers believed the religious leader to be a <u>compas-</u>

<u>sionate</u> man , compassionate to _____ .

Develop original sentences, repeating in each one a word that ends in -*ing*.

1. _____

_____

2. _____

_____

As you read, watch for sentences that follow this pattern and add them below.

_____

_____

_____

_____

_____

_____

_____

_____

_____

```
┌─────────────────────────────────────────────────────────────────┐
│  PATTERN 9a:        A VARIATION:                                  │
│                     SAME WORD REPEATED IN                         │
│                     PARALLEL STRUCTURE                            │
│                                                                   │
│   S     V    repeated key word in same position of the sentence. │
└─────────────────────────────────────────────────────────────────┘
```

EXPLANATION:

Repetitions of words may occur in other ways, of course.

1. You may repeat some effective adjective or adverb in phrases or clauses with parallel construction:

That South Pacific island is an *isolated* community, *isolated* from the values of the West, *isolated* from the spiritual heritage of the East.

2. You may repeat the same preposition in a series:

All revolutionists are negative; they are *against* things—*against* the values of the present and *against* the traditions of the past, *against* materialism and *against* mysticism, *against* taxation and representation and legislation.

3. You may repeat the same noun as the object of different prepositions:

This government is of the *people,* by the *people,* and for the *people.*

4. You may repeat the same modifying word in phrases that begin with different prepositions:

Sidney devoted his life to those *selfish* people, for their *selfish* cause, but clearly with his own *selfish* motives dominating his every action.

5. You may repeat the same intensifiers:

Audrey appeared *very* chic, *very* classic, *very* blasé.

Politicians sometimes concern themselves with *some* important issues, *some* burning questions, *some* controversy dear to their constituents.

6. You may repeat the same verb or alternative forms of the same word:

"It isn't always others who enslave us. Sometimes we let circumstances enslave us; sometimes we let routine enslave us; sometimes we let things enslave us; sometimes, with weak wills, we enslave ourselves."—Richard Evans, *Richard Evans' Quote Book*

EXAMPLES:

"Porphyria's Lover" captures a moment of time, a moment of passion, a moment of perverse indulgence.

His greatest discoveries, his greatest successes, his greatest influence upon the world's daily life came to Edison only after repeated failure.

You must find other ambitions, other goals, if your first ones are unrealistic.

The city itself sets the pace for Venetians—for their leisure, their tasks, their efforts, and their hopes.

NOTE: Observe the repetition of the pronoun *their.*

PROFESSIONAL EXAMPLES:

"The book sprawls and passes its perfect happy ending, where the lovers, at last free to marry, at last accepted by the public, at last secure that their romance will not destroy their careers, reach the final consummation of sharing a bag of popcorn at a movie."—Joan Quarm, *El Paso Herald-Post*

"Villainy is the matter; baseness is the matter; deception, fraud, conspiracy are the matter . . . ."—Charles Dickens, *David Copperfield*

"The only thing we have to fear is fear itself."—Franklin Delano Roosevelt, First Inaugural Address

"He [Richard] imagined he was walking on someone's face, anyone's face, everyone's face, anonymous faces—his face, the faces of those he hated, the faces of those he wanted to love."—Benjamin A. Saenz, "Kill the Poor," *Rio Grande Review,* Spring/Summer 1992

"You are as young as your faith, as old as your doubt, as young as your self-confidence, as old as your despair."—Stanley Ullman, fifteenth-century French essayist

"Lying awake at 2 A.M., unable to sleep because of the mattress, unable to read because of the reading lamp, unable to watch TV because of the absence of TV, I wonder whether anyone will remember me or find me, in the morning."—William Zinsser, *Lingua Franca,* March/April 1993

"Suspicion took hold, suspicion that would grow to a furious conviction."—David Nevin, *Smithsonian*

"*Next Generation's* high-class, high-tech, high-budget premiere episode (which, for a little continuity, featured a cameo by De Forest Kelley as a very ancient Dr. 'Bones' Mc Coy) was specifically engineered to smooth ruffled feathers."—Michael Logan, *TV Guide*

NOTE: The repeated, hyphenated modifiers *(high-class,* etc.) precede the subject *episode.* Also, an interrupting modifier appears within parentheses.

EXERCISES:

Expand each of the following basic sentences by repeating one of the modifying words in a phrase.

1. Your grandmother was right : there is nothing new under the sun, nothing _____ , only

_____ .

2a. But these numbers tell only part of the story, only _____

_____ , only

_____ , only

_____ .

b. (Rewrite the same sentence but this time repeat the word *part.*) But these numbers tell only part of the story, part _____

_____ , part

_____ .

3a. The western world possesses awesome amounts of virtually untapped resources , awesome _____ ,

awesome _____ .

b. (Rewrite the same sentence but repeat the word *untapped.*) The western world possesses awesome amounts of virtually untapped resources , untapped _____ , untapped

_____ .

c. (Rewrite the same sentence but this time repeat the word *resources.*) The western world possesses awesome amounts of virtually untapped resources, resources _____ ,

resources _____ ,

resources _____ ,

resources _____ .

As you read, watch for sentences that follow this pattern and add them below.

_____

_____

_____

_____

_____

_____

_____

_____

_____

_____

| <u>S   V   word</u> : | the appositive (the second naming) .
(with or without modifiers) |

EXPLANATION:

Often it is an idea, not a word, that you wish to repeat. Withholding the repetition until the end builds the sentence to a climax and provides a pattern for a forceful, emphatic appositive that concludes the sentence and practically shouts for your reader's attention. In the above pattern, the colon—because it is formal and usually comes before a rather long appositive—emphasizes this climax. Remember that the colon marks a full stop and therefore must come only after a complete statement; it tells the reader that important words or an explanation will follow.

Also, when you believe a repeated word deserves greater stress, you can make it into an appositive and signal the importance of the appositive by a preceding colon. The colon alerts readers to the importance of the word after it; note that here only a single word follows, unlike PATTERN 3, which has an entire sentence after the colon. Turn now to page 18 and contrast PATTERNS 10 and 3; after doing so, look at three similar PATTERNS—3, 10, and 10a—and note the differences in both the structures and the appropriate times when you would use them to achieve unique rhetorical effects.

EXAMPLES:

Atop the back of the lobster is a collection of trash: tiny starfish, moss, sea conchs, crabs, pieces of kelp.

Anyone left abandoned on a desert should avoid two dangers: cactus needles and rattlesnakes.

Airport thieves have a common target: unwary travelers.

PROFESSIONAL EXAMPLES:

"The Tarahumara Indians are also master hunters and gatherers, scraping an incredible array of edibles from the austere landscape: catfish, eels; the flesh of deer, opossums, wolves; insects, worms, and grubs; snakes, toads, and lizards; berries, fungi, cactuses, 13 kinds of roots, and 39 varieties of weeds."—Robert Schultheis, "Into a Canyon, Back in Time," *National Geographic Traveler,* September/October 1992

"Discover some members of Spain's unique wildlife that will amaze and inspire you: the elusive Spanish Wolf, the graceful Flamingo, the impressive Brown Bear, the majestic Imperial Eagle, the amazing Spanish Lynx."—*Lookout,* 1992

"And you could write a literary history of Britain using nothing but a succession of pubs as its points of reference: The Mermaid Tavern on London's Bread Street, for example, where Ben Jonson, Sir Walter Raleigh, and the playwrights Beaumont, Fletcher, and probably Shakespeare met; or the Cheshire Cheese on Fleet Street where William Butler Yeats used to read his poetry in a room in which Boswell, Goldsmith, and Dr. Johnson once regularly read."—Jo Durden-Smith, "Solving the British Pub Crisis," *European Travel and Life,* October 1991

"Every object [in George Washington's study at Mount Vernon] reflected an energetic and practical mind: a large desk; a handsome globe; a library that emphasized history, politics, law, agriculture, literature, and travel; a handpress for making copies of letters; a barometer and a telescope; some surveying instruments; a few guns; and a reading chair with a pedal that activated an overhead wooden fan that stirred the humid summer air and kept the flies away."—William Zinsser, "An American Icon," *National Geographic Traveler,* July/August 1992

NOTE: Since this series has internal punctuation, the items must be joined by semicolons rather than by commas.

"New Zealanders on vacation in Queenstown appear devoted to flinging themselves off high peaks and bridges: alpine skiing, tobogganing, parasailing, hang gliding, and 'bungee jumping'—that bizarre sport where you stand with one end of a long elastic (*bungee*) cord bound to your ankles and the other end to the small platform jutting out from a bridge, then dive off, trusting that the cord will halt your plunge into the river and bounce you up and down, until you come to a dangling halt."—C. D. B. Bryan, "The Last Place on Earth," *European Travel and Life,* June/July 1990

"The hair coat in the cat consists of three different types of hair: primary or guard hairs within the outer coat; awn hairs (immediate-sized hairs forming part of the primary coat); and secondary hairs (downy hairs found in the undercoat)."—John Saidla, Cornell Feline Health Center

NOTE: Once again, the series has internal punctuation and needs semicolons.

SENTENCE FOR ANALYSIS:

Analyze the following sentence, looking for repetitions, sentence patterns, punctuation, and content. In the space provided, jot down your reaction to the sentence—its length, clarity, and rhetorical effectiveness.

"Rhey avoided talk about the deceased's final year, about how he had been transfigured by drugs in a losing battle against an inoperable brain tumor, about how he was reduced from a trim, combative five-mile-a-day runner to a frail man in a wheelchair, his head swollen with chemicals, his eyes hollow with defeat and sadness."—*American Way,* January 1992

_____

_____

_____

CHECKPOINTS:

✔ Check the words *before* the colon; be sure they make a full statement (sentence).

✔ After the colon, be sure to write only a word or a phrase—not a full statement. See PATTERN 3.

EXERCISES:

Supply the missing parts for the following sentences. Each sentence should include an emphatic appositive.

1. _____ :

an "A," the grade I really had worked for .

2. (Make up a sentence with a person's name as the emphatic appositive.) _____ :

_____
(name)

3. The class elected _____

as treasurer : Jim Rutledge .

4. _____ award :

_____ , the most coveted of

all _____ distinctions .

5a. (Make up a sentence with an emphatic single-word appositive.
After the appositive use a prepositional phrase to modify it.)

_____ :

_____ .
(appositive plus prepositional phrase)

b. (Rewrite the sentence in *a* and make the emphatic appositive into
an infinitive phrase. Remember that an infinitive consists of *to* and
the base form of a verb, as in *to squirm.)*

_____ :

to _____ .
(infinitive phrase)

c. (Now, repeating the same idea as in *a* and *b* above, modify the
emphatic appositive with a word group beginning with *-ing* or an
-en or *-ed* word—that is, a *present* or *past* tense participle.)

_____ :

_____ .
(*-ing, -en,* or *-ed* word)

As you read, watch for sentences that follow this pattern and add them below.

PATTERN 10a: A VARIATION: APPOSITIVE
                    (single or pair or series) AFTER A DASH

<u>S   V   word</u> —   the appositive ....
                                (echoed idea or second naming)

EXPLANATION:

For variation, for a more informal construction, you may use a dash instead of a colon before a short, emphatic appositive at the end of a sentence. Notice that in both PATTERNS 10 and 10a, the second naming is usually climactic or emphatic. The difference is only in punctuation: a dash almost always precedes a short, climactic appositive, whereas a colon generally precedes a longer appositive. (Now contrast PATTERN 9 with PATTERN 10a.)

Study the differences in sound and emphasis that the punctuation and the length of the appositive make in the following sentences:

Adjusting to a new job requires one quality, humor.
    (common usage but not emphatic)

Adjusting to a new job requires one quality above all others—a sense of humor.
    (dramatic signaling)

Adjusting to a new situation requires one quality: humor.
    (significant pause, but not so dramatic)

Adjusting to a new job requires one quality: the ability to laugh at oneself.
    (more dramatic, more stylistically complete)

EXAMPLES:

Many traditional philosophies echo the ideas of one man—Plato.

The relatively few salmon that make it to the spawning grounds have another old tradition to deal with—male supremacy.

The grasping of seaweeds reveals the most resourceful part of the sea horse—its prehensile tail.

The muraled walls of the south side are the scene of a popular game—*rebote*, commonly known as handball.

But now there is an even more amazing machine simplifying our daily lives—the facsimile machine, better known as the FAX.

No matter how reticent the players may be, the Indian University team will always have someone with a lust for commanding center stage—their coach.

The Greeks' defeat by Alexander could have been averted if they had listened to their most astute statesman—Demosthenes, the brilliant adviser of the Athenians.

PROFESSIONAL EXAMPLES:

"Gothic cathedrals usually have at least one rose window—a composition in the round with panels like petals." —Stanley Meisler, *Smithsonian,* June 1990

"All across America there are dead utopias—Brook Farm, Oneida, Kaweah, Modern Times, Memnonia—places where dreamers pledged to plow and thresh together, to share equally in the sweat and fruits of labor, to yield their individuality or their spouses to the commune." —Henry Wiencek, *Smithsonian,* May 1992

CHECKPOINTS:

✔ Keep in mind that the second naming must be a true appositive; don't just "stick in" a dash or a colon before you get to the end of the sentence. If you do, you may simply create an error in punctuation, not a true appositive. Here is an example, lifted from a student's paper:

POOR: One class of teenagers can be labeled—students.

CORRECT: One label would fit almost any teenager—student.

✔ Remember that a dash cannot separate two complete thoughts. Avoid a "dash splice."

WRONG: Mary Shelley spent a full year at Marlow writing *Frankenstein*—her monster has survived better than some of her husband's poems.

CORRECT: Mary Shelley spent a full year at Marlow writing *Frankenstein*—creating a monster that has survived better than some of her husband's poems.

EXERCISES:

Rewrite each of the following sentences so that it ends with a dramatic appositive after a dash. You may need to add, delete, or rearrange words.

1. *War and Peace,* one of the world's masterpieces, covers Napoleon Bonaparte's crucial campaign, an invasion of Russia by the largest army ever assembled from twenty nations.

   _____

   _____

   _____

2. The thesis of *War and Peace,* as stated by Tolstoy, is that the course of the greatest historical events is determined ultimately not by military leaders, but by conventional people.

   _____

   _____

   _____

Compose or rewrite sentences as directed below:

1. (Supply the missing dramatic appositive.) The destiny of nations is controlled by the common people — _____

   _____ .

2a. (Make up a sentence ending with a dramatic single-word appostive after a dash.) _____ —

   _____ .
   (single word)

b. (Rewrite the sentence, ending it with a dramatic prepositional phrase) _____

_____ — _____
(prepositional phrase)

_____ .

c. (Again rewrite the sentence, ending it with a dramatic infinitive phrase.) _____ —

_____ .
(infinitive phrase)

d. (Now repeat the same idea, using an *-ing* or an *-en* word or phrase at the beginning of the dramatic appositive.) _____

_____ —

_____ .
(*-ing* or *-en* word here)

As you read, watch for sentences that follow this pattern and add them below.

_____

_____

_____

_____

_____

_____

_____

Modifiers

Adding modifiers is a good way to clarify a sentence that is too brief or lean. Often some key word will require additional explanation—one or more modifiers—in order to make its meaning clear. Modifiers are especially helpful if you wish to appeal to your reader's senses, to add some figurative language, or to make comparisons or allusions.

These modifiers may be single words, phrases, even clauses; they may be at the beginning, in the middle, or at the end of the sentence. They may be ideas or descriptions or figures of speech. Take two short, ineffective sentences. Make one into a modifier or a dependent clause, and then combine it with the other sentence for a stronger, clearer construction.

You will have no trouble with modifiers if you remember one fact: like leeches or magnets, they cling to the nearest possible target. Therefore, take care to avoid misplaced or dangling modifiers. If a modifier clings to the wrong target, you will have an incoherent, illogical, or ludicrous sentence.

A special use for the appositive is as a modifier for the whole sentence, not just one word. This appositive renames an idea implied or explicitly stated somewhere in the sentence.

```
PATTERN 11:        INTERRUPTING MODIFIER
                   BETWEEN S AND V


    S   ,       modifier      ,      V    .
    ───                              ───
    S   —       modifier      —      V    .
    ───                              ───
    S    ( modifier that whispers )  V    .
    ───                              ───
```

EXPLANATION:

When a modifier comes between the subject and the verb, you may use a pair of commas or a pair of dashes to separate it from the main elements of the sentence. If the modifier is merely an aside within the sentence (a kind of whisper), put parentheses around it for variety in punctuation. This modifier need not be just a single word; it may be a pair of words or even a phrase that provides additional information, as in the examples below.

In this pattern, the punctuation sets off the modifier dramatically. You would use this pattern when you believe dramatic signaling is appropriate, as you do in PATTERNS 10 and 10a. The difference in PATTERN 11 is that the word stressed is a modifier rather than an appositive. Also, note that a pair of commas, a pair of dashes, or parentheses may be chosen to set off the word, depending on the type of emphasis you want to give the modifier.

EXAMPLES:

A small drop of ink, falling like dew upon a thought, can make millions think.

A small drop of ink, falling (as Byron said) like dew upon a thought, can make millions think.

Rare meat, even though containing more natural juices than well-done meat, is chewier.

Mule deer (once common throughout North America) are now almost extinct.

Curanderos—often seen in many urban *barrios* and rural areas in the Southwest—combine herbs, massage, and prayer into a magical healing process.

Relaxation and informality are important parts of our fantasies about life in a tropical paradise; and once you get accustomed to having twenty people waiting on you hand and foot (it doesn't take very long), you no longer feel like a guest.

American fast food has certainly taken hold, especially among young people of Singapore, and steakhouses (not to mention McDonald's and Kentucky Fried Chicken) are familiar sights along Orchard Road.

PROFESSIONAL EXAMPLES:

"Scores of Chinese eating houses, sometimes with encyclopaedic menus, sometimes with provincial variations from one small district to another, are an education in themselves." —Singapore Tourist Promotion Board, Raffles City Tower

"Little San Simon Island deer—your basic American white-tailed variety—are omnipresent . . . lurking on the fringes of the compound . . . ." — "Little St. Simon Island, Georgia," *Condé-Nast Traveler*

SENTENCE FOR ANALYSIS:

In the following sentence, why did the writer use parentheses? What impact do they have on you? How important is the material within the parentheses? Note the capitalization *after* the colon.

"It is still possible to live like a maharaja (although it's not quite as comfortable as one might wish): Simply book passage on the Maharaja of Jodhpur's private railcar, the last royal train remaining in India." — *Condé Nast Traveler,* September 1992

CHECKPOINT:

✔ Remember that the punctuation marks for this pattern must go in pairs, with one mark before the modifier and a corresponding mark after it.

EXERCISES:

Add additional information and descriptions of the subjects in the following sentences by providing interrupting modifiers or other missing parts. (Review the exercises for PATTERNS 7 and 7a, to determine the difference between an interrupting appositive and an interrupting modifier before you begin this exercise.)

1. My Father's Day gift , _____ ,

_____ .

2. _____ — like the amber of a stunning topaz —

_____ .

3. _____ , distressing yet not unexpected , _____

4. The gestures of the drum major (_____

_____) were almost

_____ .

5. (Use this sentence for the exercises below.) The political candidate learned the results of the Michigan primary.

    a. (Provide **one** or **two** words ending in *-en* as the interrupting modifier.) The political candidate _____ ,

_____ , learned the results of the Michigan primary .

    b. (Provide **two** words ending in *-ing* as the interrupting modifier.) The political candidate — _____ — learned the results of the Michigan primary .

    c. (Provide a modifier in **parentheses** that whispers.) The political candidate (_____) learned the results of the Michigan primary .

As you read, watch for sentences that follow this pattern and add them below.

_____

_____

_____

_____

_____

_____

_____

_____

_____

EXPLANATION:

The modifier that interrupts the main thought expressed by the subject—verb combination may be more than merely words or phrases. It may be a full sentence—a statement, a question, or an exclamation. If it is a full sentence, do not put a period before the second dash unless the statement is a quotation. If this sentence is a question or an exclamation, however, you will need punctuation. A question mark or an exclamation point may seem strange in the middle of a sentence, but this pattern requires such punctuation.

The interrupting modifier need not always come between the subject and the verb; it may come in other places in the sentence (see the last three examples below). And notice the different signals that the punctuation gives the reader. Parentheses really say that the material enclosed is simply an aside, not very important. Dashes, however, indicate that the interrupter is important to a complete understanding of some word in the sentence.

EXAMPLES:

Juliet's famous question—early in the balcony scene she asks, "Wherefore art thou, Romeo?"—is often misunderstood; she meant not "where," but "why."

One oı Thoreau's most famous analogies—"If a man does not keep pace with his companions, perhaps it is because he hears a different drummer. Let him step to the music he hears, however measured or far away."—echoes Shakespeare's advice that we should be true to ourselves.

NOTE: Here the statement before the dash is a quotation, and the period is correct.

He jumped at the chance (too impetuously, I thought) to shoot the rapids in his kayak.

NOTE: Here the interrupting modifier comes *after* the verb.

Although the young models were standing on the rolling slopes wearing their new $500 parkas—they were pretending to know how to ski—not one of them dared to venture down the giant slalom.

Narcissus ignored Echo so completely (how could he? she was such a lovely nymph!) that she just faded away.

PROFESSIONAL EXAMPLES:

"Born just 100 years ago—his centenary was in 1988—T. E. Lawrence continues to fascinate and intrigue each new generation." —Pam Sarnoff, "The Fountains of Potency"

"For a person so notoriously outspoken in print—her quoted speech bristles with military metaphors—Cheney is remarkably reticent in person." —David Segal, "Cheney's Command," *Lingua franca,* September/October 1992

"But I have come to believe—indeed I have to believe it insofar as I believe in the validity and efficacy of art—that what comes to us first and foremost through the body, as a sensuous affective experience, is taken and transformed by the mind and self into a thing of the spirit." —George Garrett, *Whistling in the Dark,* Harcourt Brace, 1992

SENTENCE TO ANALYZE:

In the following sentence note how the writer uses parentheses to enclose both whole sentences and single modifiers. Observe also that the author makes a general comment, then follows with quotations from John Jerome's book as specific illustrations enclosed in parentheses. Do you find the punctuation distracting, helpful, or effective?

"In lively, thoughtful entries Jerome tells stories about his writing career (like the time the editor of *Esquire* summoned him in to save the October issue); ponders language ("Punctuation is nails, screws, nuts and bolts, the means by which you secure things in place."); tells how to start a book proposal ("Imagine that the book-to-be gets onto the *Times* best seller list, then write the two-line summary that would run with its listing."); exults over good reviews ("more dancing around the kitchen"); and talks about his work in progress." —"The Writing Trade," *BOMC News,* February 1992

_____

_____

_____

CHECKPOINT:

✔ Use this pattern with restraint. Otherwise your reader may think you have a "grasshopper mind" and can't finish one thought without interference from another.

EXERCISES:

Supply the missing parts for the following sentences, keeping in mind that for PATTERN 11a the modifier must be a sentence:

1. The scary movie (I know _____ !)

_____

2. Julius Caesar's famous question— "Et tu, Brute?"— _____

_____

3. My new Florida suntan— _____

_____ —seemed out of place

for January .

4. _____ (it dates back to the

1980s, at least) _____ .

5. Generally thought to be of Dutch origin, the tulip— _____

_____ —originally came

from central Asia .

As you read, watch for sentences that follow this pattern and add them below.

_____

_____

_____

_____

_____

_____

_____

_____

_____

_____

Participial phrase	,	S V	.
S V	,	Participial phrase	.

EXPLANATION:

Modifiers come in a variety of forms—single words, groups of words (phrases), even clauses. One unique kind is the participial modifier, a verb form that, used as a single word or as part of a phrase, functions as a modifier. There are three forms for participles:

> *present*   (ending in -*ing*)
>
> *past*   (normally ending in -*en* or -*ed*)
>
> *irregular*   (so *irregular* that you will have to memorize these!)
>
> EXAMPLE: Persevering, determined to succeed, driven by wanderlust, blest with discipline, the pioneers forged a civilization out of a wilderness.
>
> > *Persevering*   (present regular)
> >
> > *determined*   (past regular)
> >
> > *driven*   (past regular)
> >
> > *blest*   (past irregular)

The dictionary will help you with irregular participial forms. Remember that all participles function as adjectives, modifying nouns or words serving as nouns. Also, participial modifiers are movable; you can place them at the beginning or the end of a sentence as long as it is absolutely clear what they are modifying.

In the following sentences, note how the movable participle phrase may be shifted to various positions to create subtle changes in meaning or emphasis. Does the second example work as well as the first or third one? If you set off the participial phrase in example two with a pair of commas, what would the sentence be saying? Would its meaning change as a result of the commas? Remember that, when you set off modifiers with a pair of commas or other punctuation, you alert your reader to commentary not really needed to communicate the main message.

Guarding us with their powerful guns, the heavily armed soldiers at the Rio conference looked ominous.

The heavily armed soldiers guarding us with their powerful guns at the Rio conference looked ominous.

NOTE: Here the phrase is *restrictive* or *essential,* suggesting that specific soldiers were guarding us. See in the other two examples how the phrase is commentary and thus *non-restrictive.*

The heavily armed soldiers at the Rio conference looked ominous, guarding us with their powerful guns.

Once you understand what a participle is, PATTERN 12 is simple. It shows participial modifiers at the beginning and at the end of the sentence, though of course they may also come as interrupters at any point (see the second example above).

CAUTION: Don't dangle participles! Place them next to the word they modify. You will have no trouble with them if you remember not to "shift subjects" at the comma: the idea or person you describe in the modifying phrase, not some other person or word, must be the subject of your sentence. Inadvertent danglers sometimes result in unintentional humor or illogical statements:

Walking onto the stage, the spotlight followed the singer.

Overgrown with moss, the gardener cleaned his seed flats for spring planting. (Overgrown with moss is the participial phrase here.)

The three boys tried to steal my bike while going on an errand.

The man in the advertisement is shown standing in the middle of a stream holding an ax surrounded by trees.

When browned and bubbling, remove the pie from the oven

See examples below for modifiers that don't dangle.

EXAMPLES:

Chaucer's monk was removed from the ideal occupant of a monastery, given as he was to such pleasures as hunting, dressing in fine clothes, and eating like a gourmet.

NOTE: *Given* is the participle here.

Overwhelmed by the tear gas, the rioters groped their way toward the fountain to wash their eyes.

The sun pushes through the early morning fog over the New York skyline and the Brooklyn Bridge, inspiring people with a desire to invent and create.

Printed in Old English and bound in real leather, the new edition of *Beowulf* was too expensive for the family to buy.

NOTE: *Printed* and *bound* are the participles here.

PROFESSIONAL EXAMPLES:

"May through September the city goes light, bright, and fanciful, animated by outdoor cafes . . . and colorful sun umbrellas that sway along the shoreline." —David Downie, "Helsinki," *Travel and Life,* March 1991

"Wet-eyed, dumbstruck by his performance, I pulled a five-dollar bill out of my wallet and dropped that into the paper bag." —Robert Fulghum, *All I really Need to Know I Learned in Kindergarten*

SENTENCE FOR ANALYSIS:

Locate in the following sentences the participial modifiers. Are they rhetorically effective?

Appearing on television talk shows, crisscrossing the country on the campus lecture circuit, invited to be on the programs of important symposia, fad theorists and former criminals become the darlings of our society before we forget and discard them for others.

_____

_____

_____

EXERCISES:

Try these exercises:

1. (Rewrite the following sentence, beginning it with an *-ed* word.) If you water your African violets carefully, they will burst into bloom.

_____

_____

2. (Rewrite the following sentence, beginning it with an *-ed* or *-en* word.) The underdog team, the Mets, beat the Hawks, but the Hawks won the championship cup in May. _____

_____

3. (Supply the missing words in this sentence. Begin with an *-ing* word.) _____ , the prisoner escaped to freedom .

4. (Begin the following sentence with an *-ed* word. Follow the *-ed* word with one *-ly* modifier.) _____

_____ , the child finally dozed off to sleep .

5. (Supply the missing words in the sentence. Begin with an *-ing* word. Follow the *-ing* word with an *-ly* word.) _____

_____ , the sparrow darted from the lower branch to the top of the tree .

6. (Rewrite the following sentence with a participial phrase at the *end.*) The residents of the apartment obeyed the water restriction rule only because they watered the lawn on Thursdays. _____

_____

_____

7 (Supply the missing words in this sentence. Begin the missing word group with an *-ing* word.) Spring weather always brightens my spirits _____ ing

_____ .

As you read, watch for sentences that follow this pattern and add them below.

PATTERN 13: A SINGLE MODIFIER OUT OF PLACE FOR EMPHASIS

Modifier   ,   S   V
         (modifier may be in other positions)

EXPLANATION:

If you wish to place additional emphasis on any modifier, put it somewhere other than its normal place in the sentence. Sometimes in this new position the modifier seems so normal that it sounds clear without a comma; at other times, you *must* have a comma to keep the reader from misinterpreting your sentence. For example:

> As a whole, people tend to be happy.

> (Otherwise, "As a whole people . . . .")

> To begin with, some ideas are difficult.

> (To begin with some ideas?)

Sometimes a single word such as *before, inside,* or *below* may look like a preposition instead of an adverb if you forget the comma in a sentence like this one:

> Inside, the child was noisy.

Now look what internal rumblings you create when you have no comma:

> Inside the child was noisy.

If a modifier is clearly an adverb, however, you may not need the comma:

> Later the child was quiet.

Using this pattern may help you to avoid another pitfall in writing sentences—the split infinitive. In the following sentence *occasionally* would be better at the beginning than where it is, separating the two parts of the infinitive. and *further* should follow *illustrate.*

> Francesca liked *to occasionally wade* in the neighbor's pool.

> The professor tried *to further illustrate* the point of the essay.

EXAMPLES:

Below, the traffic looked like a necklace of ants.

Frantically, the young mother called for help.

Frantic, the young mother rushed out the door with the baby in her arms.

All afternoon the aficionados sweltered on the sunny side of the corrida, watching the matador from Mexico City, their latest idol.

The general demanded absolute obedience, instant and unquestioning.

The autumn leaves, burgundy red and fiery orange, showered down like a cascade of butterflies.

NOTE: This is PATTERN 11.

PROFESSIONAL EXAMPLES:

"There are hotels that are merely places to stay, and then (rarely) there are Hotels with a capital *H*." —Bob Schultheis, *National Geographic Traveler,* September/October 1992

"Writers, ghettoized, fell into their own subcultures, often forming parallel 'professional' organizations and holding their own conferences and conventions." —Jay Parini, "The Theory and Practice of Literature," *The Chronicle of Higher Education,* September 1992

NOTE: This sentence, lifted out of context from an article about conventions, may sound odd to you. The word *ghettoized,* an uncommon past participle out of normal order, stresses the various groups at the convention and the ghettolike quality of separateness.

SENTENCES FOR ANALYSIS:

1. In the following sentence look for ways that David Segal conveys his emotional stance (*tone*). Occasionally authors can show an emotional reaction to their material. In describing the manner of Lynne Cheney, Segal interrupts the second clause with the modifier *well.* How does this carefully placed *well* suggest Segal's attitude toward Cheney's policies?

"Cheney denies that she meddles; in my interview with her, she describes herself as, well, helpful." —David Segal, *Lingua Franca*

_____

_____

_____

2. How is *well* used, stylistically, in the dependent clause of this sentence?

"And there is a certain spaciousness, a 'swagger' in these works, that seems, well, American." —J. E. Vacha, *American Heritage,* September 1992

_____

_____

_____

EXERCISES:

Revise each of the following sentences so that a modifier you want to emphasize comes at the beginning.

1. Rodeos began as rough-and-ready contests among rival cowboys to settle long festering differences. _____

_____

_____

2. Rodeos are a multi-million-dollar business now in all parts of the West. _____

_____

_____

3. Many rodeo events lead to black eyes, broken ribs, dislocated shoulders, or even worse injuries. _____

_____

_____

4. Saddle-bronc riding, which requires coordination, balance, timing, is naturally considered the classic rodeo event. _____

_____

_____

5. The inmates of the Huntsville prison organize a well-publicized, rough-and-tumble rodeo every October. _____

_____

_____

As you read, watch for sentences that follow this pattern and add them below.

_____

_____

_____

_____

_____

_____

_____

_____

_____

Inversions

Not all sentences need to start with the traditional subject—verb combination. For variety you may wish to invert the normal order by beginning the sentence with a modifier out of its normal place; complements or direct objects may occasionally precede the subject. These inverted units may be single words, phrases, or dependent clauses.

Be wary of any inverted pattern, however. It may lead to awkwardness if your writing is undisciplined. Inverting the natural order should always result in a graceful sentence, not one that seems forced or suggests an intentional gimmick. Just as every sentence should seem natural, almost inevitable in its arrangement, so too must the one that departs from traditional sentence order. Try not to call attention deliberately to any inversion; make it fit into the context gracefully. Aim for sentences that possess the magic of variety, yes; but remember that too much variety, too obviously achieved, may be worse than none at all. (Turn to PATTERN 15a for further explanation.)

PATTERN 14: PREPOSITIONAL PHRASE BEFORE S—V

Prepositional phrase   S   V   (or   V   S) .

EXPLANATION:

Before trying this pattern, remember what a preposition is. The very name indicates its function: it has a *"pre-*position." The *pre* means that it comes before an object, which is necessary to make a prepositional phrase. In other words, a preposition never occurs alone because it must show the relationship between the word it modifies and its own object. For example, consider a box and a pencil. Where can you put the pencil in relation to the box? It might be "on the box" or "under the box," "beyond the box" or "near the box," "inside the box" or "beside the box." Can you think of other prepositions?

For this pattern, put one or more prepositional phrases at the beginning of the sentence, making sure that the inversion emphasizes the modifying phrase without sounding awkward. Only your ear will tell you whether to put a comma after it; will the reader need the punctuation for each reading? If so, provide it.

For example, these sentences *must* have commas:

> After that, time had no meaning for him.
> Beyond this, Rex can probably never go.
> (Not "after that time" or "beyond this Rex.")

These sentences do well without a comma:

> Until next summer there will be no more swimming.
> During the winter months Tom worked as a trapper.

EXAMPLES:

Down the field and through the tacklers ran the Heisman Trophy winner.

Despite his master's degree in world trade and economics, the only job Chester could get was making change in an Atlantic City casino.

With slow and stately cadence the honor guard entered the Windsor Castle grounds.

Into the arena rushed the brave bulls to defy death and the matador.

In all the forest no creature stirred.

Under the care of Bishop Jean Baptist Lamy, Sante Fe, New Mexico, became an important, thriving village.

Down there the desert has a peculiar horror.

NOTE: In this sentence, *there,* almost always an adverb, functions as a noun.

Up and down these chasms the traveler and his mules clamber as best they can.

PROFESSIONAL EXAMPLES:

"Into the valley of death / Rode the six hundred." —Alfred, Lord Tennyson, "The Charge of the Light Brigade"

NOTE: Here the example comes from poetry, but you can see how easily PATTERN 14 can be adapted to prose.

"In the past, restoring a frescoed wall involved little more than covering the crack and dabbing fresh paint on the surface . . . ." — George Armstrong, *Modern Maturity*

"From his tongue flowed speech sweeter than honey." —Homer, *Iliad*

"By their own follies they perished, the fools." —Homer, *Iliad*

CHECKPOINT:

✔ Be aware that sometimes a comma is necessary after the prepositional phrase, sometimes not. Let the sound and meaning of your sentence guide you.

EXERCISES:

Supply the missing parts of these sentences, which include introductory prepositional phrases. Try to use *more* than one or two words in each blank.

1. To the athletes _____ , the new NCAA

regulations represented _____ .

2. _____ stood the farmer holding a

loaded shot gun .

3. After _____ yet before

_____ , the veterans soon realized

that _____ .

4. In _____ by

_____ of _____

_____ the Persian cat

_____ .

5. With a clear _____ of

the principles of _____ ,

a student _____

As you read, watch for sentences that follow this pattern and add them below.

<table>
<tr><td colspan="2">PATTERN 15:</td><td colspan="2">OBJECT OR COMPLEMENT
BEFORE S—V</td></tr>
<tr><td>Object</td><td>or</td><td>Subject complement</td><td>S   V   .</td></tr>
</table>

EXPLANATION:

Occasionally you may wish to invert and thereby stress some part of the sentence that ordinarily comes after the verb (the direct object or the subject complement). These may go at the beginning of the sentence instead of in their normal positions. Any inversion adds invisible italics or stress to the part of the sentence you write first. When you use PATTERN 15, always read your inversion aloud to be sure that it sounds graceful in context, that it blends well with the other sentences around it. Here, as in PATTERN 14, only the sound and rhythm of the sentence will indicate whether you need a comma; there are no rules.

EXAMPLES:

This example has the direct object before the subject—verb combination:

> His kind of sarcasm I do not like.

These examples have a subject complement before the subject—verb combination:

> **SC**   **DO**
> Content he can remain with his money; true friends he will never have.

> No enemy of metaphor is Amy Lowell.

> Famous and wealthy an English professor will never be.

> "Up went the steps, bang went the door, round whirled the wheels, and off they rattled."
> > —Charles Dickens, *The Old Curiosity Shop*

NOTE: Adverbs are stressed in this inversion.

CHECKPOINT:

✔ Inversions are easy to do out of context, just for the exercise. But in a setting with your other sentences, you need to take care that they sound natural, not forced or awkward. Therefore use them sparingly, and then only for special emphasis.

EXERCISES:

Supply the missing information in these inverted sentences:

1. _____ was Cinderella, but

then neither were her stepsisters .

2. _____ a child seldom

understands .

3. _____ the Heisman Trophy

may always be, yet it remains a goal of all college football players .

4. The Congressional Medal of Honor every soldier _____

_____ ; however, few

_____ .

5. _____ solar power

might well become .

As you read, watch for sentences that follow this pattern and add them

below.

PATTERN 15a: COMPLETE INVERSION
OF NORMAL PATTERN

Object OR Complement OR Modifier   V   S   .

EXPLANATION:

The standard English syntax is

subject—verb

subject—verb—modifier

subject—verb—completer (direct object or subject complement).

Completely reversing the order of these sentence parts will create an emphasis and a rhythm you can achieve in no other way:

verb—subject

modifier—verb—subject

completer—verb—subject.

This pattern will add spice to your prose; but too many reversals, like too much garlic or cayenne pepper, can be overpowering. So restrain yourself; don't overuse this pattern. It will probably fit better into dramatic statements or poetic prose passages than into business letters or laboratory reports.

EXAMPLES:

Westward the country was free;   Mod S V C
westward, therefore, lay their hopes;   Mod V S
westward flew their dreams. The West became   Mod V S
for everyone the promised land of   Prep. phrase
milk and honey   out of place
                                                  between V
                                                  and SC

From the guru's prophecy radiated a faith that ultimately all would be well.

Down the street and through the mist stumbled the unfamiliar figure.

Even more significant have been the criticisms about the quality of life in our affluent society.

In "The English Mail Coach" DeQuincey has a sentence with PATTERNS 15 and 15a: "But craven he was not: sudden had been the call upon him and sudden was his answer to the call."

From his years of suffering came eventual understanding and compassion.

Sleek and silver-haired the managers may be, but by and large they tend to be men whose principal concerns involve money.

PROFESSIONAL EXAMPLE:

"Never before have we had so little time to do so much."—Franklin Delano Roosevelt, "Fireside Chat," February 1942

CHECKPOINTS:

✔ Remember that this pattern must never offend the ear by sounding awkward or stilted.

✔ Test your sentence by reading it aloud. How does it sound? Is it consistent with your tone? Does it fit neatly into the context?

EXERCISES:

Revise each of the following sentences so that you create a complete inversion of the normal subject—verb pattern. You may have to add, delete, or alter some of the wording.

1. The gallant marine did not fear death. _____

_____

2. When we fly to Europe, we must visit London and Paris and Rome.

_____

_____

3. Marching against the Mexican army, the brave Texans chanted,

"Remember the Alamo!" _____

_____

_____

4. A human being's power of choice, either for good or evil, is

boundless. _____

5. The dreamer and the doer live side by side in each of us.

_____

As you read, watch for sentences that follow this pattern and add them
below.

_____

_____

_____

_____

_____

_____

_____

_____

_____

An assortment of patterns

```
PATTERN 16:          PAIRED CONSTRUCTIONS

Not only    S    V   , but also          S    V
                         (The also may be omitted.)
Just as     S    V   , so too            S    V      .
                         (may be so also or simply so)
If not               , at least              *
The more    S    V   , the more          S    V
                         (may be the less)
The former  S    V   , the latter        S    V      .
```

EXPLANATION:

Some words work in pairs; for example, *either* takes an *or; not only* takes *but also.* These *correlative conjunctions* link words, phrases, or clauses that are similar in construction. The patterns in the box above illustrate some common phrases used for paired constructions that may occur in simple or in compound sentences. You will find these structures particularly helpful in making a comparison or a contrast.

Whenever you use the pattern marked with an asterisk, remember to make both parts of the construction parallel; that is, give them both the same grammatical structure and rhythm:

Two nouns: if not *praise,* at least not *blame*

Two prepositions: if not *in* the park, at least not *in* the back alley

Two adjectives: if not *apple,* at least *pumpkin* pie

EXAMPLES:

American tourists must realize that violations of laws in China are serious not only because they flaunt traditional codes of behavior but also because they reflect contempt for Oriental culture.

Just as slavery divided North and South, so the Indian Wars of the nineteenth century divided East and West.

---

* Note that the *if not . . . at least* construction joins individual grammatical units, not complete clauses.

Reluctantly, every dieter looks for a favorable verdict from the bathroom scale: if not a pound less, at least not an ounce more.

The more the Texas Ranger searched through the Hill Country, the more elusive the trail of the train robbers became.

The more I saw films by that director, the less I liked his work.

Kai and Ernst were two of my favorite ski instructors: the former taught me downhill racing; the latter helped carry me to the hospital where Dr. Alexander set my fractured arm.

PROFESSIONAL EXAMPLES:

"To accomplish great things, we must not only act, but also dream: not only plan, but also believe."—Anatole France

"Just as a good painting is almost always about more than it depicts, so does its historical value extend beyond its subject."—"The Winter Art Show," *American Heritage,* December 1990

"And just as classical demigod heroes, like the Greek Achilles or the Trojan Aeneas, could not stoop to standard weapons from the common armory but required spear, sword, shield forged on a divine anvil, so too did the Celtic heroes."—Graeme Fife, *Arthur the King*

CHECKPOINTS:

✔ Remember that pair means "two." Be sure to supply the second part of the construction; don't give the reader a signal suggesting two items and then provide only one. To say "Not only is she pretty" and then say no more is to leave your reader confused.

MORE PAIRS: The following list of correlative conjunctions may further aid you in developing this pattern:

whether . . . or	*so . . . that*
such . . . that	*not only . . . more than that*
both .. and	*as . . . as*
neither . . . nor	*not so . . . as*

CAUTION: Put both conjunctions of a pair in logical places so that what follows each one will be parallel.

WRONG: The prisoner was | not only | found guilty

of murder | but also | of robbery.

(no parallel verb here)

CORRECT: The prisoner was found guilty

| not only | of robbery

| but also | of murder.

(parallel construction;
better order for climax, too.)

WRONG: I | not only | forgot my keys

| but also | my purse.

(no parallel verb)

CORRECT: I forgot | not only | my keys

| but also | my purse.

EXERCISES:

Complete the following sentences with logically paired constructions:

1. The _____ Robert tried to please

his fiancee , the _____ dissatisfied

_____ .

2. The _____ a parent spends on a

child's Christmas present , the _____

_____ the child _____

_____ .

3. Just as National Public Radio provides new opportunities to _____

_____ , so it

_____ .

4. The Mercedes Benz's beauty is _____

_____ in its design _____

_____ in its function .

5. _____ if not the

Pattersons , at least their neighbors .

Correct the following errors in parallelism:

1. Robert not only forgot to invite two of his fraternity brothers to the wedding but also his banker. _____

_____

_____

2. His father-in-law offered John nothing, neither a position with the brokerage firm or a monthly allowance._____

_____

_____

3. During the convocation ceremony the spectators smiled both at their friends and relatives or the funny-looking Grand Marshal, who proudly carried the university banner. _____

_____

_____

4. The committee abandoned plans for the senior examination because neither the Board of Regents or the system lawyers believed it would prove anything or be worth the trouble. _____

_____

_____

As you read, watch for sentences that follow this pattern and add them below.

_____

_____

_____

_____

_____

_____

_____

_____

_____

A "this, not that" or "not this but that" construction   .

in some place other than the verb position

EXPLANATION:

This type of paired construction—the simple contrast—illustrates the differences between two ideas and usually involves a reversal. This simple contrast by reversal may be dramatically emphatic or may simply reinforce an ironic purpose. Unlike PATTERN 16, this one does *not* involve correlative conjunctions. If you want to show a reversal in the middle of your statement, simply say something is *"this,* not *that"* or *"not this,* but *that."* Punctuation marks—especially commas, dashes, or parentheses—will help indicate a break in your sentence and establish your point of reversal or contrast.

EXAMPLES:

By just a quirk of fate (not by deliberate choice) Columbus landed in the Caribbean, not the Gulf of Mexico; in the West Indies, not the East Indies.

For some hummingbirds, migration involves a much smaller range, measured in hundreds, not thousands, of miles.

The symphony conductor was convinced that it was she, not the orchestra, and certainly not the music, that the audience had come to honor.

Genius, not stupidity, has limits.

Most students have to learn that "meanings" are in people, not in messages.

The judge asked for acquittal—not conviction.

PROFESSIONAL EXAMPLES:

I believe that man will not merely endure; he will prevail."—William Faulkner, Nobel Prize Speech, Stockholm, Sweden

"Count the nights by stars, not shadows."—"Leanin' Tree," Boulder, Colorado

"Liberal education settles issues in terms of idealism, not interest; in terms of right, not force."—Dinesh D'Souza, *Illiberal Education*

"Water belongs to the land, not to the farmers."—Nick Inman and Clara Villanueva, *Lookout,* April 1992

"Custer raises his saber no longer (the 7th Cavalry didn't carry sabers into battle); his hair doesn't flow in the hot wind (he had cut off his hair, and there was not even a breeze that day); nor is he clad all in buckskins (he had stripped off his jacket in the heat); nor is he standing (not if they shot him in the ribs by the river); nor do the Sioux race around him on their horses (most were dismounted); nor do they charge him with war clubs (most were sensibly shooting their bows and rifles from distant tangles of sage)."—Andrew Ward, "The Little Bighorn," *American Heritage,* April 1992

NOTE: This sentence, a variation of PATTERN 11a, states various misconceptions about General Custer and the Sioux, then debunks them with the information in parentheses.

"Astrology is a disease, not a science."—Maimonides, *Laws of Repentance*

"Do not let us speak of darker days; let us speak rather of sterner days."—Winston Churchill, "Address at Harrow School," October 1941

EXERCISES:

Using the following sentences for words and ideas, create contrasting "this, not that" or "not this but that" sentences. Use dashes and parentheses as well as commas to establish your point of reversal.

1. Saddle-bronc riding is the classic rodeo event even though many spectators prefer the dangerous Brahma-bull-riding contests.

_____

_____

_____

2. Although Jules resembled a skilled ski coach he was actually a male model displaying a $900 ski ensemble._____

_____

_____

3. With horror Sandra realized that Jerrell was a werewolf; he had been masquerading as a royal prince of Transylvania. _____

_____

_____

Create complete sentences, using for each one the indicated point of contrast.

1. _____ — not

romance — _____ .

2. _____ , not freedom .

3. _____ (not just

milk and a sandwich) _____

_____.

Create a point of contrast for each of the following incomplete structures:

1. The argument was the result of two clashing philosophies —

not _____ .

2. The ballerina could wear the dainty satin slippers , but not

_____ .

3. No _____ , Rafael made a

number of tactless remarks.

4. The voters did not want dissolute politicians ; _____

_____ .

5. A student wants to know the truth , not merely _____

_____ .

As you read, watch for sentences that follow this pattern and add them below.

_____

_____

_____

_____

_____

_____

_____

_____

_____

_____

PATTERN 17:   DEPENDENT CLAUSE
(in a "sentence slot")
AS SUBJECT **OR** OBJECT
OR COMPLEMENT

S [dependent clause as subject]   V   .

S   V   [dependent clause as object or comp.]   .

EXPLANATION:

As you learn to vary your sentence structures, alternating simple with more complex ones, you will find this pattern especially helpful in achieving variety and style. Although a sophisticated pattern, it is (strangely enough) quite common in speech; it is easy to use in your written work, too, if you understand that the dependent clause is merely a part (subject, object, or complement) of the independent clause.

The dependent clauses in this pattern, which serve as nouns, will begin with one of the following words:

who, whom, which, that, what, why, where, when, how

after which will come the subject—verb of the dependent clause. If one of these introductory words IS the subject, it will need only a verb after it.

EXAMPLES:

[*How he could fail*] is a mystery to me.
(subject of verb *is*)

He became [*what he had long aspired to be.*]
(complement after *became*)

[*What man cannot imagine*], he cannot create.
(object of *can create* in this "inverted" sentence)

Juliet never realizes [*why her decision to drink the sleeping potion is irrational*].
(object of verb *realizes*)

[*Why many highly literate people continue to watch insipid soap operas on television*] constantly amazes writers, producers, even directors.
(subject of *amazes*)

[*Who assassinated President Kennedy*] continues to be a hotly debated subject.
(introductory word is subject)

[*That he was a werewolf*] became obvious when his fingernails turned into claws.
(subject of verb *became*)

PROFESSIONAL EXAMPLES:

"And so my fellow Americans, ask not
    [clause as DO]
[what your country can do for you];
      [clause as DO]
ask [what you can do for your country]."—John F. Kennedy

    [clause as OBJ. of prep. *for*]
"He for [whom this bell tolls] may be so ill,
      [clause as DO]
as that he knows not [it tolls for him]"—John Donne, Meditation XVII

    [clause as DO]
"[Why Leonardo rejected the technique] we may never know."—George Armstrong, *Modern Maturity*

"What it is, I'm still not exactly sure."—"Letter from London," *European Travel and Life*

    [clause as SC]
"For that, I insist, is not [what pubs are for]."—"Solving the British Pub Crisis: Know When to Say When," *European Travel and Life*

"When an individual is taken into custody or otherwise deprived of his freedom by the authorities and is subjected to questioning. . . he must be warned prior to any questioning that he has the right to remain silent, that anything he says can be used against him in a court of law, that he has the right to the presence of an attorney, and that if he cannot afford an attorney one will be appointed for him prior to any questioning if he so desires—Chief Justice Earl Warren, *Miranda v. Arizona,* 384 United States 436, 1965

NOTE: The italics should alert you to the dependent clauses.

CHECKPOINT:

✔ Remember that the dependent clause can never stand alone; it is only a portion of your sentence. Therefore don't put a period before or after it because you will create an awkward fragment. For instance, these two examples are wrong:

> With horror she realized that he was a philanderer. Why her mother had a low opinion of him.

> Juliet never realizes why her decision to drink the sleeping potion is irrational. Which explains why she drinks it.

How would you correct these errors?

EXERCISES:

Insert a dependent clause in each of the blanks. Be sure each clause has a subject—verb combination.

1. After many years of research the scientist realized that _____

_____ .

2. Why _____ the

members of the social club will never understand .

3. What swimmers _____

_____ , they can definitely accomplish .

4. That _____

became clearer to me as I thought over his answer .

5. How often she _____

_____ shocked not only _____

_____ but also _____

_____ .

As you read, watch for sentences that follow this pattern and add them below.

_____

_____

_____

_____

_____

_____

_____

_____

_____

```
PATTERN 18:          ABSOLUTE CONSTRUCTION
                     (noun plus participle)
                     ANYWHERE IN SENTENCE


Absolute construction      ,      S      V      .
.................................
 S  ,       absolute construction  ,      V           .
               OR
___                              ___
               OR
      (                             )
```

EXPLANATION:

What exactly is an absolute construction? It is a noun or pronoun plus a participle with no grammatical connection to the independent clause. What's absolute about it? Only its independence, its lack of any grammatical connection to the sentence. It modifies the entire sentence, not a single word. At home in any part of the sentence, an absolute construction is a separate entity that can function in either of two ways: (1) to explain a cause or condition or (2) to provide details about a focal point in the independent clause. Maybe these constructions are called "absolute" because they are absolutely different from anything else in English grammar; they are not dependent clauses because they have no verbs, and for the same reason they could never be independent clauses.

> ABSOLUTE: His blanket being torn, Linus cried on Charlie Brown's shoulder.

> DEPENDENT CLAUSE: Because his blanket was torn, Linus cried on Charlie Brown's shoulder.

If carefully used, this pattern will be one of your most helpful devices for varying sentence structure. If tossed into a sentence cavalierly, however, it may create inexcusable awkwardness. Try not to force this construction; instead, look for places in your paragraph where it would seem natural.

You may work with irregular participles (*torn* and *burnt* here):

> His blanket torn and his finger burnt, Linus cried on Charlie Brown's shoulder.

Or you can work with present participles:

> The American economy, God willing, will soon return to normal.

His early efforts failing, Teddy tried a new approach to the calculus problem.

If you wish, you may even use several participles and then contradict all of them with a contrasting adjective, as the following sentence illustrates:

Casesar continued his march through Gaul, his army tattered, exhausted, hardened—but victorious.

EXAMPLES:

The walls being blank, the new tenant—an unemployed artist—promptly set about covering all of them in a mural of orange, vermillion, and yellow.

I plan to sail to Tahiti (my pension permitting) as soon as I retire from this company.

We had our Memorial Day picnic after all, the rain having stopped before sunset.

All things considered, the situation seems favorable.

What the dog reflects is his master's true emotion, admitted or not.

Buffalo abounding, the pioneers often killed many more than they needed for food—the greatest wildlife slaughter the world has ever known.

PROFESSIONAL EXAMPLES:

"She sat back on the bed, her head bowed, her lips moving feverishly, her eyes rising only to scan the walls."—Anne Rice, *Interview with the Vampire*

"The storm, its fury abated, lights the way."—John Cullen Murphy, "Prince Valiant," December 1992

"Various legal requirements aside, a living trust is a truly personal instrument."—Ameritrust pamphlet

NOTE: In this absolute construction, the participle set is implied after the word *requirements.*

CHECKPOINT:

 Keep in mind that the absolute construction, because it has no grammatical connection with the sentence, must always have some punctuation. Use a comma after an absolute phrase at the beginning of the sentence or before one at the end. Such a phrase in the middle of the sentence must be enclosed by a pair of commas, dashes, or parentheses.

EXERCISES:

Provide an absolute construction for the blank in each of the following sentences:

1. The tantalizing aromas from my grandmother's kitchen linger

in my memory, all of them _____

_____ .

2. The little boy stood beside the swimming pool, his eyes

_____ .

3. Their nostrils _____ , the race

horses _____ .

4. The sounds of the airport—jets _____

_____ , people _____ , the

public address system _____ — suggest

the excitement, frustration, and chaos of the place

5. The accordion player's hands raced over the keys, his right

hand _____ , his left hand

_____ .

As you read, watch for sentences that follow this pattern and add them below.

_____

_____

_____

_____

_____

_____

_____

_____

_____

_____

```
┌──────────────────────────────────────────────────────────┐
│  PATTERN 19:        THE SHORT, SIMPLE SENTENCE FOR         │
│                     RELIEF OR DRAMATIC EFFECT              │
│                                                            │
│              S              V                              │
│         _____                    │
└──────────────────────────────────────────────────────────┘
```

EXPLANATION:

This pattern for a short sentence can provide intense clarity, but brevity alone will not make it dramatic. Actually, this pattern will be effective only

> when you employ it deliberately after several
>   long sentences,
> or when you let it more or less summarize what
>   you have just said,
> or when you let it provide transition between
>   two or more ideas.

"All was lost" or "Thus it ended" may not look very startling here, but in the appropriate context such a terse sentence may be quite dramatic. After a series of long, involved sentences, a statement with only a few words can arrest the readers' attention, make them pause, shock them into considering the ideas in the longer sentences that precede it. This pattern may, indeed, condense or point up what you have taken several longer sentences to explain.

Developing your style involves practice and training your ear to hear "a good turn of the phrase."

Polonius knew this.

EXAMPLES:

Well, I wonder.	But then it happened.
Days passed.	Just consider this.
It was magical.	Don't laugh.
That's not my style.	That's okay.
Perseverance pays.	I think not.
It's time to move on.	And this is true.
All efforts failed.	He was unbeatable.
Everything changed.	Let's talk.

PROFESSIONAL EXAMPLES:

"Jesus wept."—The Bible

"The buck stops here."—sign on Harry Truman's desk

"Know thyself."—Plutarch, *Lives*

"People sense that."—William Zinsser, *National Geographic Traveler,* July/August 1992

> NOTE: This sentence concluded a seven-page article.

"Hello, sucker!"—Texas [Mary Louise Cecilia] Guinan

"And they do."—Charles Krauthammer, *Time,* August 1992

"I came, I saw, I conquered."—Julius Caesar

"Call me Ishmael." (the dramatic first sentence in *Moby Dick*)

NOTE: Try to imagine the kind of context that would make these sentences dramatic and effective. You might also consider how experienced writers, such as Charles Dickens, join a number of short, balanced thoughts into one long sentence that could have been broken down into a series of short sentences, brief and dramatic. But imagine how choppy the opening of *Tale of Two Cities* would have sounded if Dickens had peppered the first paragraph with short sentences rather than one long sentence, with a series of parallel and balanced parts:

"It was the best of times, it was the worst of times, it was the age of wisdom, it was the age of foolishness, it was the epoch of belief, it was the epoch of incredulity, it was the season of Light, it was the season of Darkness, it was the spring of hope, it was the winter of despair, we had everything before us, we had nothing before us, we were all going direct to Heaven, we were all going direct the other way—in short, the period was so far like the present period, that some of its noisiest authorities insisted on its being received, for good or for evil, in the superlative degree of comparison only."—Charles Dickens, *A Tale of Two Cities*

CHECKPOINTS:

✔ Recognize that length is not the criterion here.

✔ Don't think that sentences such as "I like petunias" or "Children laugh" fit this pattern just because they are short. They might, of course, but only in the proper context.

✔ Look in your reading to discover how professional writers employ this technique of short sentences for special effects.

✔ This pattern is best when it is emphatic, points up a contrast, or summarizes dramatically.

PATTERN 19a:

A SHORT QUESTION
FOR DRAMATIC EFFECT

(Interrogative word) auxiliary verb S V	?
(Interrogative word standing alone)	?
(Question based solely on intonation	?
Auxiliary verb S V	?

EXPLANATION:

This pattern may involve either of two basic constructions: a question that begins with an interrogative word, or a statement that becomes a question through intonation (pitch or tone) of voice.

It is effective in several places:

in the introduction to arouse the reader's interest,

as a topic sentence to introduce a paragraph;

within the paragraph to provide variety;

between paragraphs to provide transition;

at the end to provide a thought-provoking conclusion.

When you write, look in these five places to discover where a question could serve some desired effect. Provoke your readers with staccato-like questions, wake them up, make them pause and think, make them ask *why* or *wherefore* about your subject.

EXAMPLES:

What caused the change?	How did she cope?
Then why did he?	What comes next?
And why not?	What if E.T. calls?
Well, who cares?	When will it end?

The following examples of questions suggested by intonation are more common in conversation than in formal prose. Imagine how the voice rises at the end of each question.

That's her mother?

You made an *A* in Esch's class?

James flunked modern dance?

Remember trolleys?

PROFESSIONAL EXAMPLES:

"Hand me the pliers, will you?"—James Trefil, *Smithsonian,* August 1992

"Or will it?"—James Trefil, *Smithsonian,* August 1992

"Who can give law to lovers?"—Boethius, *Consolation of Philosophy,* Book 12

"Who will bell the cat?"—William Langland, *Piers the Plowman*

CHECKPOINTS:

✔ Recognize that questions need to be handled carefully to be effective.

✔ Avoid scattering them around just because they are easy; make them serve some purpose, such as to arouse curiosity, to stimulate interest, to lead the reader into some specific idea about your subject.

EXERCISES:

In whatever you are reading, look for the short, dramatic question. Copy the sentence here and add a comment about its function within the overall context; recall that there are at least five effects, and try to find an example of each.

1. Example: _____

_____

Comment: _____

_____

2. Example: _____

_____

Comment: _____

_____

3. Example: _____

_____

Comment: _____

_____

4. Example: _____

_____

Comment: _____

_____

5. Example: _____

_____

Comment: _____

_____

PATTERN 20: THE DELIBERATE FRAGMENT

Merely a part of a sentence

EXPLANATION:

The mere mention of the word *fragment* chills the blood of some conservative teachers; but a master stylist, ironically enough, often relies on brief sentence fragments to give emphasis and a sense of immediacy to his or her prose. The deliberate fragment should create a dramatic effect within a paragraph; it should serve some purpose, such as forcing the reader to look backward. If it doesn't, don't use it. Often only the context in which the fragment would appear can tell you whether to put it in or leave it out. Used sparingly, the fragment can be as effective as the rhetorical question or the short, dramatic sentence. Used injudiciously, it is simply another ineffective gimmick.

EXAMPLES:

Try a fragment

● in a description—

I wish you could have known the Southwest in the early days. The way it really was. The way the land seemed to reach out forever. And those endless blue stretches of sky! The incredible clarity of air which made distance an illusion. I wish I could make you see it so you would understand my nostalgia, nostalgia and sorrow for a wonder that is no more.

● for transition—

Now, on with the story.
But to get back to the subject.
So much for that.
Next? The crucial question to be answered.
First, the nuts and bolts.
Meanwhile.

● for indicating conclusions—

Fair enough.   All too late.
No matter.   Fine.

- in structuring a question or an answer—

    But how?

    And why not?
    What then? Nothing.
    Based on logic? Hardly!
    Where and when and why?

- for making exclamations and for emphasis—

    What a price to pay!
    Probably not!
    Never!
    The next step—martyrdom.
    Shameful nonsense.

- for making explanations—

    All to no avail.
    But for short journeys.

- and sometimes in aphorisms or fragments of clichés—

    The more the merrier for them, too.
    But there's the rub.
    Early to bed!
    Absolute power corrupting once more.

PROFESSIONAL EXAMPLES:

"What a mistake!"—Frederic Vitoux, *European Travel and Life,* December/January 1991

"A final anecdote."—Frederic Vitoux, *European Travel and Life,* December/January 1991

NOTE: Here Vitoux uses the deliberate fragment to provide transition to a new paragraph.

"Running again."—David Nevin, *Smithsonian,* May 1992

NOTE: Here another writer uses the deliberate fragment to provide transition to a new paragraph.

CHECKPOINTS:

✔ If you are in the habit of writing fragmentary sentences, don't think that you have already mastered this pattern!

✔ Use this pattern, like PATTERNS 19 and 19a, only as a deliberate styling device. It should never be merely an accident or a mistake in sentence structure or punctuation.

CAUTION: Use PATTERNS 19, 19a, and 20 sparingly and precisely.

EXERCISES:

In your reading look for highly styled, deliberate fragments used for dramatic effect. Copy the fragment and add a brief comment about its function or purpose.

1. Example: _____

_____

Comment: _____

_____

2. Example: _____

_____

Comment: _____

_____

3. Example: _____

_____

Comment: _____

_____

4. Example: _____

_____

Comment: _____

_____

5. Example: _____

_____

Comment: _____

_____

CHAPTER 3

SENTENCES GROW

At this stage you are ready to make sentences grow . . . and grow some more.

Now that you are familiar with some of the more complex patterns in CHAPTER 2, let's combine two or more of them to create additional variety in your sentences. Only a few examples of sentence combinations appear in this chapter, but you will discover many more possibilities as you experiment on your own, still remembering these cautions: always try to write a sentence that fits into the total context; never force a construction simply for the sake of variety.

Don't be afraid to be creative. Experiment not only with your own favorite patterns from CHAPTER 2 but also with others, with new ones you will discover in your reading or create in your own writing. When you learn to maneuver sentence patterns, when you feel at ease manipulating words, then you will be a master of sentence structure if not yet a master stylist.

Now to discover what patterns combine well—

Combining the patterns—ten ways

1. The compound sentence with a colon combines effectively with a series and the repetition of a key term (PATTERNS 3, 4, 9a).

    > To the Victorians much in life was sacred: marriage was sacred, the family circle was sacred, society was sacred, the British empire was sacred.

2. Repetition also combines well with a dependent clause as an interrupting modifier (PATTERNS 9, 11).

    > The experiences of the past—because they are experiences of the past—too seldom guide our actions today.

3. A dependent clause as complement combines well with an appositive at the end of a sentence after a colon and a series with balanced pairs (PATTERNS 17, 10, 5).

    > Ted became what he had long aspired to be: a master of magic and illusion, of hypnotism and sleight-of-hand tricks.

4. The series without a conjunction and the repetition of a key term combine well with the introductory appositive and an inversion of any kind (PATTERNS 4, 9, 9a, 15a).

    > The generation that was too young to remember a depression, too young to remember World War II, too young even to vote— from that generation came America's soldiers for Southeast Asia.

5. The compound sentence without a conjunction can combine with repetitions and series (PATTERNS 1, 4, 4a, 9).

    > Books of elegiac poetry had always stirred Jason; they made him think of music, music that sang of ancient glories, of brave men, of the things they loved and hated and died for.

6. Introductory appositives may be written as dependent clauses and the repetition of a key term followed by a question for dramatic effect (PATTERNS 6, 8, 9, 19a).

    > That there are too many people, that overcrowding causes social, economic, and political problems, that human fellowship and compassion wear thin in such an environment—these are problems facing the inner city today, problems that eventually young people must solve. But how will they?

7. An inversion of the sentence pattern may also include a prepositional phrase before the subject—verb combination within a compound sentence (PATTERNS 1, 14, 15a).

> Around Jay were men of various nationalities; to none of them could he ever really relate.

8. A pair of dependent clauses as direct objects will work well with paired words, a series without a conjunction, an interrupting modifier with dashes, and a repetition of the same word in a parallel construction (PATTERNS 4, 11, 9a, 16, 17).

> The ambassador found that not only was America experiencing painful expansion and costly social upheavals—over foreign policy, racial disorder, economic priorities—but also that the nation was facing the threat of a national paralysis of will, a paralysis of faith.

9. An interrupting modifier that is itself a sentence may go well with another type of modifier (PATTERNS 11, 11a).

> His family, a respected conservative family ruled mainly by several maiden aunts—his father had died when he was a child—had been scandalized at the thought that their young heir wanted to devote his entire life to hot-rod racing and roller-derby competition.

10. After a long, involved compound sentence without a conjunction, a fragment with a repeated key word and then a fragmentary question may be very effective (PATTERNS 1, 4a, 9a, 20).

> The ecology-awareness movement aims at balance and wholeness and health in our environment; it wants to assure a proper place in the scheme of things for people, for plants, and for animals. Not an exclusive place for either one, just a proper place for each. But how?

SENTENCES FOR ANALYSIS:

The following sentences from professional writers combine several patterns you learned in CHAPTER 2. Identify them, looking for their special characteristics. Pay particular attention to series structures, length, balance, the amount and appropriateness of detail, effective punctuation, and the appearance of sentences within other sentences. More important, look for patterns that you can adapt to your own style.

1. The 190E Mercedes Benz is a car to respect, to value, to appreciate; the 500SL is a car to adore.

_____

_____

2. See how the writer has used an out-of-breath repetition at the end of this sentence. Notice that it contains an allusion to Bugsy Siegel, one of the early developers of Las Vegas.

"The lights rippled, rolled, darted, sequenced their way through fantastical patterns against the black, empty screen of beyond, millions and millions of lights, more than crazy Bugsy could have imagined, far more than someone who's never spent a night in Las Vegas could ever, ever, ever—even in the wildest reaches of dreams—hope to comprehend."—Kathryn Marshall, *American Way,* September 1991

_____

_____

3. "Everything for which Japan is known exists in Kyoto: The modern rush and bother and sex and sleaze and chrome and high-technology excitement are all there; but alongside the finest and most exquisite food, the most classical and revered exponents and teachers of various schools of tea ceremony, of flower arranging, of kabuke and noh, the most renowned teachings of the art of the geisha, the best in damascene, lacquer, in handmade paper, in dolls, the art of sand raking, of potting, of making brocades, of arranging the Kimono, of fashioning tiny gardens with moss, of diverting small streams—in short, everything, for those of an alliterative bent, from Zen to Zaitech."—Simon Winchester, "Kyoto," *Condé Nast Traveler,* February 1992

_____

_____

4. "Imagine a macadam track from San Francisco to Wichita, barely two lanes wide with no markings on most stretches, serving the following traffic: ten-ton trucks constantly jockeying to pass one another, buses with riders hanging on for their lives, big cars called Ambassadors that lumber along like tanks, camel trains, oxcarts, cycle rickshaws, wandering cows, motor scooters, bicycles and pedestrians, including the occasional itinerant with a dancing bear on a leash."—Constance Bond, *Smithsonian,* May 1992

---

5. "Here is an 1872 brochure for weather vanes: horses, roosters, cows, eagles, plows, fish, hogs, swans, cannon, shovels, flags, peacocks, stars."—*Smithsonian,* April 1991

---

6. "After the Lincoln County War [New Mexico in 1878], Billy [the Kid] failed to live up to his potential—not as a respectable, law-abiding citizen, not as a Robin Hood battling against injustice, not as a cold-blooded killer, not even as the premier outlaw of all time."—Robert Utley, "Billy the Kid Country," *American Heritage,* April 1991

---

7. Writing in the *Washington Post,* Henry Allen raised press bashing to a level rarely heard since [Gen. William T.] Sherman: "The Persian Gulf press briefings are making reporters look like fools, nitpickers and egomaniacs; like dilettantes who have spent exactly none of their lives on the end of a gun or even a shovel; dinner party commandos, slouching inquisitors, collegiate spitball artists; people who have never been in a fistfight much less combat; a whining, self-righteous, upper-middle-class mob jostling for whatever tiny flakes of fame may settle on their shoulders like some sort of Pulitzer Prize dandruff."—Peter Andrews, "The Media and the Military," *American Heritage,* July–August 1991

---

8. "American families in shorts, bickering and road-weary, climb and descend the macadam path to Last Stand Hill, the women stumping along with their aim-and-shoots, the children fidgeting with their Nintendo Gameboys, the men in caps explaining with the instant authority of sports fans—'Now listen to me, kids'—that the marble stones that punctuate the battlefield mark where the troopers are buried (they don't exactly), that the fighting was hand to hand (it wasn't), that the Sioux tricked Custer (they didn't), that he is buried beneath the monument on Custer Hill (if he is, it's inadvertent; he's supposed to be buried at West Point, but some believe that in 1877 a burial detail may have shipped the wrong set of disinterred remains, in which case an enlisted man has been impersonating an officer for more than a century)."—Andrew Ward, "The Little Bighorn," *American Heritage,* April 1992

---

9. "It [the maze] has been used for courting (a favorite place for Tudor trysts); for religious processions (the line of worshippers never once crossing); as a form of contemplation and penance (monks supposedly shuffling along the stony paths on their knees); and, even now, for fertility rites—a gameskeeper in Hampshire is always having to move couples on from one particular maze site."—Martin O'Brien, "Garden-Variety Puzzles," *Travel and Life*

---

10. "Whether the Southwest will develop a distinct culture I do not know. I only know that if a distinctly Southwestern culture is developed, it will employ cattle brands and no signs of the zodiac to ornament the facades of its buildings; that its gardens will be made beautiful by native mountain laurel as well as by English boxwood; that it will paint with the colors of the Painted Desert as well as with the colors of the Aegean; that is, biographers will have to understand Sam Houston better than they understand John Quincy Adams; that is, actors on the stage will cultivate the drawl of the old-time Texans rather than the broad *a*'s of Boston; and that the aroma of jasmine and bluebonnets, the golden fragility of the *retama,* the sting of a dry norther, the lonely howl of the coyote, and the pulsing silence of places where machines do not murder quietude— such things will appeal to the senses through the rhythems [*sic*] of its poets."—J. Frank Dobie, quoted in Clark Kimball, *The Southwest Printer,* Texas Western Press, 1990

_____

_____

Expanding sentences

Frequently writers find that a simple sentence with a single subject and a verb is too brief or lean, that the meaning is not complete or clear. What is missing is one or more modifiers that will add explanations, descriptions, specific details, amplifications, or supporting materials to make the sentence meaningful to the reader. Thus, in order to make a point, the writer *adds* to the sentence. Modifiers help the reader visualize and illustrate the generalization expressed in the basic sentence. These modifiers may be words, phrases, or clauses that appear at the beginning, the middle, or the end of the sentence; they may also modify one another.

Think of the basic idea, the primary kernel sentence, as the first level of writing and the modifiers added for clarity as the second or the third or the fourth level of writing. Each successive level is related to the one immediately above it and is related to the basic sentence by the intervening modifiers, some subordinating, some coordinating. Later on, as you acquire more experience in writing, look for a generalization or an abstract word in your sentence—clear to you but possibly not to your reader—that will require you to shift and backtrack, adding modifiers at different levels to help the reader comprehend fully the meaning you have in mind. Francis Christensen, *Notes Toward a New Rhetoric* (New York: Harper and Row, 1967), named this type of expanded sentence the "cumulative sentence." In it the base sentence of main subject and main verb with their "bound modifiers" (those that cannot move about) *accumulates* additions. To the base one adds "free modifiers" (those that can move about) that enrich the sentence and create a feeling of motion. A later description of the Christensen method appears in *A New Rhetoric* (New York: Harper and Row, 1976).

Study the examples below and notice how modifiers on different levels in the subject slot help expand the sentence and clarify its meaning.

LEVEL ONE:　the basic slots for any sentence (S—V)

<u>Whooping</u> <u>cranes</u> <u>fly</u>. (the "kernel sentence," according to Francis Christensen)

Now, on different levels add modifiers to the subject.

LEVEL TWO: (the first modifiers): may come before or after subject or verb:

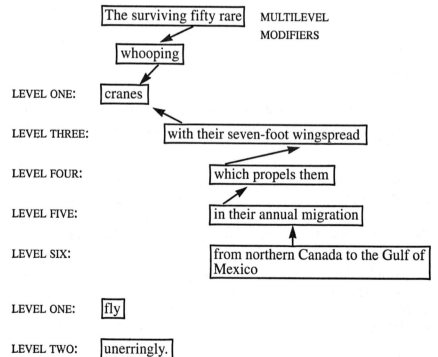

Now add more modifiers on different levels in the verb slot:

LEVEL ONE (the basic S—V) : Whooping cranes fly.

LEVEL TWO: modifiers for the verb:

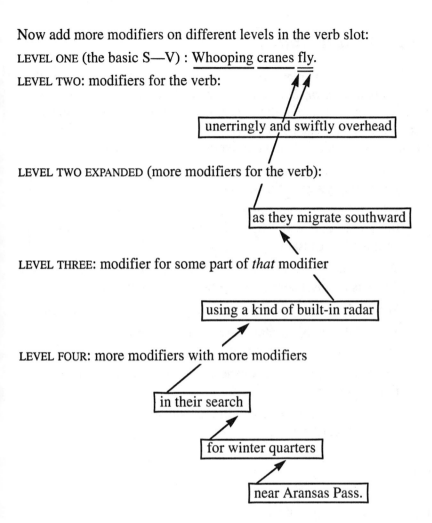

unerringly and swiftly overhead

LEVEL TWO EXPANDED (more modifiers for the verb):

as they migrate southward

LEVEL THREE: modifier for some part of *that* modifier

using a kind of built-in radar

LEVEL FOUR: more modifiers with more modifiers

in their search

for winter quarters

near Aransas Pass.

Now see what modifiers can do to a basic sentence:

The surviving fifty rare whooping cranes, with their seven-foot wing-spread, which propels them in their annual migration from northern Canada to the Gulf of Mexico, fly unerringly and swiftly overhead as they migrate southward using a kind of built-in radar in their search for winter quarters near Aransas Pass.

Myths about coordinators

Some writers believe it's inappropriate to begin a sentence with one of the seven coordinators: *and, or, but, nor, for, so,* and *yet.* Nevertheless, many experienced writers *do* use coordinators now and then to begin sentences and to link ideas. Review the coordinators and their meanings; then observe how professional writers use them effectively to begin sentences.

and   What follows is an addition to the information previously given, implying continuation of a thought.

but   What follows is something unexpected—an exception, or something contrary to the first thought. *But* implies opposition or contrast in a causal way.

for   What follows is a reason why something did or did not occur. There is a causal connection between two thoughts.

nor   What follows is a continuation of a previous negative thought.

or   What follows is an alternative, another opinion. *Or* suggests only one alternative at a time.

so   What follows is a consequence, a result, or a reason for something to occur.

yet   What follows implies a conditional situation; something is true despite apparent obstacles.

EXAMPLES:

And now you're on your own.

And in the middle of the Cole Porter tune, too.

Or you could take an earlier flight and arrive in Huntsville about 4:15 P.M.

Or you can take an alternative route and avoid the traffic.

But peace of mind remains as elusive as ever.

But he, too, survives.

Nor did she give a reason.

Nor can I explain.

Yet he is little remembered.

Yet there are exceptions to this pattern.

So that's it.

So we'll start here.

For it was magical.

For the champion was unbeatable.

PROFESSIONAL EXAMPLES:

"And that's the way it is."—Walter Cronkite, CBS Evening News sign-off line.

"And then what?"— "They Say It Can't Happen Here," *California,* July 1990

NOTE: This is the final line of a long article.

"But now I'm a big boy too and I can do anything and anything and anything."—Ernest Hemingway, *The Garden of Eden*

EXERCISES:

As you read, observe how professional writers often use the short, simple sentence for dramatic effect. Copy the sentence here and add a comment about its function in the overall context—to provide transition, to give variety, to shock the reader, and so on.

1. Example: _____

_____

Comment: _____

_____

2. Example: _____

_____

Comment: _____

_____

3. Example: _____

_____

Comment: _____

_____

4. Example: _____

_____

Comment: _____

_____

5. Example: _____

_____

Comment: _____

_____

A sentence with special emphasis: the periodic sentence

A special pattern helpful in creating suspense is the _periodic sentence._ Unlike the _loose_ or _cumulative sentence,_ which begins with the main clause and continues with supporting details, the periodic sentence delays statements of the central idea until the period at the end. The important thought is deliberately withheld from the reader to create a special climax.

Every sentence has points of emphasis where you place known and unknown information. In other words, your reader will be looking in particular places for something new. It is sometimes best to delay giving this unknown information until the end of the sentence, the primary point of emphasis. A periodic sentence enables you to place the unknown at a strategically powerful point. It's important not to bury new information in the middle, where it will be forgotten.

A second point of emphasis in the sentence is near the beginning, in the subject slot. In this position you place known information, with which your reader is likely to be familiar, because it is not so crucial as what's new.

Few of your sentences will be periodic. In fact, the majority will be loosely structured. Sometimes, though, you will want to withhold unfamiliar information to create suspense. Place the less important items first, then gradually move toward the more important, with the most vital bit saved for a climactic ending. Here is a humorous sentence that illustrates the periodic structure: "I attribute such success as I have had to the use of the periodic sentence."

Now analyze this example:

"While caravan after caravan winds its weary way across the desert sands, bringing precious cargo from far inland marts to the bazaars that are the meeting-places of the East and West, most of the camels in these trains announce their coming through the melodious tinkling of brass bells."—brochure on camel bells of Sarna

How did the writer create suspense? What crucial bit of information was withheld until the very end? What is the purpose of the details in the long clause that begins the sentence?

Now contrast the loose structure of the first sentence below with the periodic structure of the second:

If the residents don't object, the planned nuclear facility will be constructed close to the lake.

The planned nuclear facility will be constructed close to the lake, if the residents don't object.

SENTENCES FOR ANALYSIS:

Here are other periodic sentences for analysis. Keep in mind the characteristics of the pattern and the questions posed above:

1. "From the deserts of Arizona to the Baltic coastline of Sweden; from Italy to India; from Chile to Celtic Britain; from wavering Bronze Age rock carvings and medieval stone-and-turf designs to the more recent and the more formal garden variety built of

evergreens such as yew and holly, the pattern of the maze has appeared throughout history with mystifying regularity in a score of unrelated cultures."—Martin O'Brien, "Garden-Variety Puzzles," *Travel and Life*

_____

_____

2. "Sketch a simple picture of azure waters, gentle breezes, and a protected anchorage; add a wash of tropical sunset colors—and you have a portrait of Cruz Bay."—Kenneth Brower, *National Geographic Traveler,* September/October 1992

_____

_____

3. "She never gives up. Her blue hair waved, circles of rouge on her wrinkled cheeks, lipstick etching the lines around her mouth, still moisturizing her skin nightly, still corseted, she dies."—Una Stannard, "The Mask of Beauty," *A Woman's Place*

_____

_____

4. "From Stettin in the Baltic to Trieste in the Adriatic, an iron curtain has descended across the continent."—Winston Churchill, Westminster College, Fulton, Missouri, March 1946

_____

_____

CHAPTER 4

FIGURATIVE LANGUAGE
IN SENTENCES

Figurative language helps words say more and mean more than their literal meanings convey. It demands from the reader an understanding of the many connotations a word may have, an ability to picture or realize the image behind the figure of speech. It also demands something from the writer: avoiding the colorless cliché. Once you understand what the various figures of speech are, once you master their "patterns," you will have no trouble thinking up original ones of your own.

Figures of speech

SIMILE:

A simile is a stated comparison between essentially unlike things, things from different classes. You must have one of the following connectives in every simile: like, as, than, or a verb such as seems. A simile says that two things are similar when they are not really alike at all.

EXAMPLES:

It's about as easy as striking a match on a mirror.

Since the disasters at Chernobyl and Three Mile Island, the threat of total annihilation has roosted, like a vulture in a tree, in Western man's awareness.

The money is expected to multiply like randy bunnies.

Here's an extended simile:

"The oil boom is like a phone call from a lost and forgotten lover; not entirely welcome, a reminder of good times that turned sour, of the end of innocence, of harsh truths learned and years irretrievably gone, of how easy it is to make a terrible mistake and how foolish it is to think that things will last forever."—Paul Burka, "Boom Town," *Texas Monthly,* December 1992

In the following similes the writer uses objects to convey measurements and compare unlike things:

"The $300 million *Majesty of the Seas* passenger megaship with a five-story atrium is as tall as the Statue of Liberty and nearly three football fields long."—*Condé Nast Traveler,* August 1992

Casanova found his mistresses' eyes were nothing like the sun. (This simile also makes an allusion to Shakespeare's Sonnet CXXX.)

METAPHOR:

A metaphor is an implied comparison. It is implied because you do not say that something is "like" or "as" another thing; you simply say that one thing IS something else. (A is B.) As with similes, here again, the two things being compared must be unlike things from different classes.

There are two types of metaphors.

TYPE 1:

The "A equals B" type uses two terms.

The sky is a blue tapestry.

The dragonfly is a blue thread hovering over the pool.

TYPE 2:

The single-word metaphor implies or suggests a comparison.

a. *verbs:* Almost any sports page will yield a rich harvest of these verbs with picture-making power.

The young rookie of the Orlando Magic skyrocketed to fame.

The quarterback blasted through the line of Nebraska's defense.

The fans came unglued and jumped up in a frenzy of excitement.

Dr. J operated on his opponents in the NBA finals.

b. *nouns:* The image or picture of comparison is implied in a noun, which names one thing by calling it another; for example, see the word "harvest" in the preceding sentence explaining verbs.

When the news anchor was hired, the television producers throught she might be another loose cannon.

The Arkansas defense line-up was a brick wall—impenetrable and invulnerable.

The quarterback crossed the line into the Promised Land, giving Ohio State six more points and a Rose Bowl win.

"Fashion is architecture: it is a matter of proportion."—Coco Chanel

c. *adjectives:* Adjectives may also imply comparisons; they describe something in terms that no reader should ever take literally.

Cynthia's feline movements clawed into Harold's composure. (Here, both "feline" and "clawed" are metaphors, suggesting something catlike about Cynthia.)

"Every slaughtered syllable is a kindness to your reader," declared the lecturer addressing the budding young journalists.

CHECKPOINTS: Don't "mix" your images in a metaphor. Look at these ghastly creations!

They stepped forth into the sea of matrimony and found it a very rocky road.

The "ship of state" might be off its keel; it might sink or flounder or get off course without a firm hand at the helm, but it could never bog down in a storm of red tape or be the leader of the team or surge ahead in second gear.

ANALOGY:

An analogy is really only an extended metaphor or simile. Analogy is an attempt to compare at length two objects from different classes; a classic analogy compares the human heart to a mechanical pump, for example or the eye to a camera. This type of comparison carried to its extreme conclusion will, of course, be illogical because in no analogy will the various parts of the two unlike objects be completely comparable.

Analogy, however, does help you to clarify some comparison you are trying to make; if appropriate and not far-fetched, it will help you to sustain a clarifying comparison throughout a short paragraph or even a long, extended piece of prose. Analogies should help you to enrich your writing, to interpret some meaning or significance about your main points, to reflect your particular way of thinking about things, to add wit and charm to your style.

EXAMPLES:

> The New York Public Library might hold the key to your future; it unlocks many doors to knowledge; it opens the way to numerous opportunities. (This would be merely metaphor unless you extended it a little further.)
>
> The human brain in some ways resembles a computer. (Now, go on—complete the analogy by showing how.)
>
> Life is like the movies: there are many kinds of plots, but you should be the director of your own script. (Does this suggest how you might discuss life as tragedy, comedy, melodrama, adventure?)
>
> To the new student the college campus is like a forest—all trees, each indistinguishable from the other and each an obstacle in his or her path. (Extend this analogy by describing how the student finds the way through the "forest" and comes to know the name—and function—of each "tree.")

An *extended analogy* sustains a comparison for several sentences, at times even for a whole paragraph. Even someone writing to clients in a business letter may use this writing technique effectively, as Margit White does in the following paragraph:

> "Being invested in the stockmarkets is a little bit like being a surfer at the beach. Whether you have your money in a Mutual Funds of stocks, a diversified portfolio of individual stocks or a Quantum account, it is all the same. You spend a lot of time sitting on your surfboard bobbing up and down

with the ebb and flow of small wavelets. But when the big wave comes, you are on your board positioned and ready for a glorious ride."—Prudential Securities *Client Letter,* January 1992

Now look at another analogy describing a landscape and comparing it to music. Does this analogy work? Can you see the comparisons suggested? Is the paragraph overwritten to the point of absurdity, or is it poignant and dramatic? What precise reaction do you have to it?

"It's a symphonic road, beginning with an andante among open hills, dropping into the somber adagio of the moist, dark redwood forest, winding its way back up through a scherzo of brighter glens and vales, and finally breaking into an allegro con brio climax of light, height, and distance, a counterpoint of long windy hillsides, hemispheric silver-barked oaks, and miles of a vibrating sea."—Peter Garrison, "Riding the Edge," *Condé Nast Traveler,* September 1992

_____

_____

_____

CHECKPOINT: Never rely on an analogy as proof in logic or argument. An analogy is simply an imaginative comparison of two essentially different things.

ALLUSION:

Allusion is another way of making a comparison; it suggests a similarity between what you are writing about and something that your reader has read before or heard about. The success of the allusion, of course, will depend on whether you strike a responsive chord in your reader's memory.

Allusions, richly connotative or symbolic, always suggest more than the words say. Because they are rich with overtones, your writing benefits by conjuring up for your readers associations from their past.

If you want to allude to something, let a word, phrase, or even your very style suggest a similarity between the subject and some other idea, a similarity real or imaginary. Success with allusions depends in part on your readers; after all, they must be able to recognize what you are alluding to. So choose allusions that will fit your audience as well as the context of your paper.

Remember that obscure allusions will cloud communication, but that appropriate ones will enable you to say more in fewer words. Try to use fresh allusions, for stale ones that have become clichés will merely bore your reader.

Common referents are history, the Bible, mythology, literature, popular personalities. In fact, a whole group of words entered the language first as allusions to persons well known in life or literature: a political maverick, a boycott, sandwiches, the little Corsican, a Mae West life jacket, an Achilles heel. How many allusions can you find in popular advertising? Or in book titles? Or in popular music?

Grapes of Wrath and *East of Eden* (both allude to the Bible)

Tender Is the Night (alludes to Keats's nightingale ode)

The Sun Also Rises (alludes to *Ecclesiastes*)

Leave Her to Heaven (alludes to *Hamlet*)

Wonderland (alludes to *Alice in Wonderland*)

Can you add other titles to the list?

EXAMPLES:

> Even if you have miles to go, you should never abandon a project without finishing it.
> (alludes to Robert Frost's "Stopping by Woods on a Snowy Evening")

> Deciding that a man's reach must exceed his grasp, Charlie decided to continue trying for top billing on the marquee.
> (alludes to Robert Browning's "Andrea del Sarto")

> Flee now; pray later.
> (In style, this should remind the reader of the familiar "Fly now; pay later" advertising slogan.)

> The omnipresent ticking of the clock on the wall made him feel chained to time.
> (alludes to Shelley's "Adonais")

The 1939 movie version of *The Wizard of Oz* is a popular source of allusion even today; note how the following examples recall scenes from the film:

> "Toto, I have a feeling that we're not in Kansas any more."

> "I could have clicked my heels together three times, but that would have put me in Kansas."—Robert Wagner dialog from *Love Among Thieves*

Here are four more examples of allusions:

> "[Suddenly, hearing] a rustling behind me, I whirled, feeling like Stanley about to meet Livingston."—*Condé Nast Traveler,* July 1992

> She played the perfect Barbie to his Ken.

> "The captain welcomed guests at the door with a novocaine smile designed by Barnum and Bailey."—*Lear's,* November 1990

> Wipe that Cheshire cat grin off your face.

PERSONIFICATION:

Used more frequently in poetry than in prose, personification gives human characteristics (like weeping or laughing) to inanimate objects or abstractions. It invests them with feelings or human attributes to create striking visual images. Abstract concepts, such as love, freedom, and time; things; or plants and flowers are often personified—Queen Anne's lace, baby's breath. Children's literature is full of personification—talking rabbits and bears and lions—Winnie the Pooh, the Cheshire Cat, the White Rabbit.

EXAMPLES:

> "Indigo shadows yawn eastward, stretching."—*El Paso,* April 1991

> Sunflowers nodded west in the afternoon sun.

> The Canadian Rockies vault into the clouds.

> The storm screamed defiance.

> "Dogs say cats love too much . ."—Alastair Reid

> "O Rose, thou art sick!"—William Blake, "The Sick Rose'

IRONY:

Perhaps the most useful figurative device from poetry and oral delivery is *irony*—the concealing of intended meaning in words that convey the opposite meaning. Ironic language presents a discrepancy between what is real and what is intended. You have heard compliments that were actually veiled criticism; the tone of a speaker's delivery conveys the real meaning. Try pronouncing "He's no fool," conveying different meanings with the same words but different intonations. Ironical remarks are softer than harsher, sarcastic speech. In sarcasm both speaker and listener know the real meaning of the message, whereas in irony meaning is subtler and less biting.

In prose, irony can be a powerful weapon. Jonathan Swift expertly attacked the Irish Catholics in his ironical "A Modest Proposal." Here he presents a wholly unthinkable answer to overpopulation—that children of the Irish poor be sold, at the age of one year, to provide "a most delicious, nourishing, and wholesome food" for wealthy purchasers. Swift advances this suggestion in logic so rigid and technically flawless that readers, while outraged, find themselves reluctantly appreciating his closing statements:

> "I profess in the sincerity of my heart that I have not the least personal interest in endeavoring to promote this necessary work, having no other good than the public good of my country, by advancing our trade, providing for infants, relieving the poor, and giving some pleasure to the rich. I have no children by which I can propose to get a single penny; the youngest being nine years old, and my wife past childbearing."

HYPERBOLE AND UNDERSTATEMENT:

Two special types of irony—apparent in both prose and poetry—are useful in communicating a message imaginatively: *hyperbole* (overstatement) and *litotes* (understatement). A bold, deliberately exaggerated statement is hyperbolic. The statement is an exaggeration that stresses the truth, but the writer does not expect the statement to be believed. Ironic in context, hyperbole can produce a fanciful effect or something comic or absurd. The speaker in Andrew Marvell's "To His Coy Mistress" uses hyperbole to present a "good line" to his beloved, suggesting that if they had all the time in the world he would adore her patiently and lavishly:

> "An hundred years should go to praise / Thine eyes, and on thy forehead gaze; / Two hundred to adore each breast, / But thirty thousand to the rest."

Try adding a hyperbolic one-liner to add humor to your message. After six hours of steady rain, you might write, "Wonderful day, isn't it?" Or in describing a large cocktail party, you might try to impress your audience by recalling, "There were millions of people there, at least two hundred of my dearest, closest friends!"

By contrast, understatement deliberately says less than what is actually intended. The speaker or writer offers us the message by stating the negative or opposite. From this seeming contradiction comes an emphatic statement that is the heart of the message. Saying of a very wise person "She's no fool" helps stress the woman's intelligence through the understatement. You might write an elaborate description of a fine meal, then underplay the excellence by saying "not bad." Note how Christopher Johns underplays the horror of a drink in which a poisonous snake floats:

> "A raw fish meal is called sashimi, and the ideal accompaniment to it is considered to be some double-distilled sake in the bottling of which a live Marmushi has been added. A Marmushi is a poisonous snake. I will spare the reader further details."—Christopher Johns, "Ah So!" The Journal of the International Wine and Food Society, February 1980.

Further reading

If you need additional information or more complete descriptions of figurative language in poetry and prose, you may consult one of the following standard reference works:

Barnet, Sylvan, Morton Berman, and William Burto. *A Dictionary of Literary, Dramatic, and Cinematic Terms.* 2nd ed. Boston: Little, Brown, and Company, 1971.

Fowler, H. W. *A Dictionary of Modern English Usage.* 2nd rev. ed. New York: Oxford University Press, 1987.

Guth, Hans P. and Gabriele L. Rico. *Discovering Poetry.* Englewood Cliffs, NJ: Prentice Hall, 1993.

Holman, C. Hugh. *A Handbook to Literature.* 5th ed. New York: Oxford University Press, 1987.

Hunter, J. Paul. *The Norton Introduction to Poetry.* 4th ed. New York: Norton, 1991.

Kennedy X. J. *Introduction to Poetry.* 7th ed. New York: Harper Collins, 1990.

Perrine, Laurence and Thomas Arp. *Sound and Sense.* 8th ed. New York: Harcourt Brace, 1992.

CHAPTER 5

THE TWENTY PATTERNS—
IN PRINT

TOUGH COUNTRY*

from *Tularosa* by C. L. Sonnichsen

SENTENCE
PATTERNS

The Tularosa country is a parched desert where everything, from cactus to cowman, carries a weapon of some sort, and the only creatures who sleep with both eyes closed are dead.

11

In all the sun-scorched and sand-blasted reaches of the Southwest there is no grimmer region. Only the fierce and the rugged can live here—prickly pear and mesquite; rattlesnake and tarantula. True, Texas cattlemen made the cow a native of the region seventy-five years ago, but she would have voted against the step if she had been asked.

14

10a

5

From the beginning this lonesome valley has been a laboratory for developing endurance, a stern school specializing in just one subject: the Science of Doing Without.

14

10

Everything has been done to promote the success of the experiments. There is almost no water; no shade. High mountain walls all around keep out the tenderfeet. On the west, screening off the Rio Grande valley with its green fields and busy highways, great ridges of limestone and granite—Franklin and Organ; San

9a

14

12

Andres and Oscuro—heave and roll northward from El   5 and 7
Paso. Across the valley to the eastward, shutting off   14
the oases along the Pecos, the Hueco mountains merge
with the pine-cloaked Sacramentos, and these give way
to Sierra Blanca and Jicarilla, with 12,000-foot Sierra   12
Blanca Peak soaring in naked majesty over all.

The Tularosa country lies between the ranges, a
great pocket of sand, sun, and sparse vegetation thirty
miles wide, more or less, and over two hundred miles
long. The Jumanos Mesa, named for a long-vanished
tribe of Indians, gives it a northern boundary. To the   11
south it merges with the Chihuahua Desert which push-   11
es far down into Mexico.

Seen from the tops of the screening ranges, it   14
looks like a flat, gray-green, sun-flooded expanse of
nothing, impressive only because the eye can travel a   12
hundred miles and more in one leap. Near at hand it is   4
full of surprises. The northern end of the valley is a little less parched. Grass still grows tall on Carrizozo
Flat, and bean farmers have plowed up the country
around Claunch. Nearby, two prehistoric lava flows
cover the land with an appalling jumble of volcanic   13
rock known locally as the *malpais.*

South of the lava flows, the vast gypsum deposits
called the White Sands spread out in a deathly, glitter-
ing world of pure white which edges eastward a few
inches each year, threatening in a few millennia to   12
swallow up everything as far as the Sacramentos.

Sometimes the valley floor heaves in sand dunes;   1
sometimes it breaks into red hummocks, each one   9a 18
crowned with the delicate green leaves and lethal
thorns of a mesquite bush. There are broad swales
where the yuccas grow in groves—leprous alkali flats
where even the sturdy greasewood can barely hold its
own—long inclines of tall grama grass where the
foothills rise to the knees of the mountains—and

countless acres of prickly pear and *lechuguilla* and rabbit brush. *4a*

A harsh, forbidding country, appalling to newcomers from gentler regions. But it has its moments of intense beauty. Sunrise and sunset are magic times. Under a full moon, that lonely, whispering waste is transformed into an austere corner of fairyland. The belated traveler catches his breath when the tender fingers of dawn pick out the tiny black shapes of the pine trees far above him on the top of the Sacramentos. One does not forget the Organs blackening against the sunset, swathed in a veil of lilac shadows—the eerie gleam of the white sands at moonrise—a swarthy cloud dissolving in a column of rain, the froth of impact showing white at its foot while all round the sun shines serenely on.

20
19

14

12
4 (*with dashes*)
12
18

The yucca is a thorny and cantankerous object, but in the spring it puts up a ten-foot stalk which explodes in a mass of creamy-white blossoms. And so it is with other sullen citizens of the desert when their time comes: the prickly pear with its rich yellow flower, the desert willow dripping with pendent pink and lavender, little pincushion cacti robing themselves in mauve petals more gorgeous than roses, the ocotillo shrouding its savage spines in tiny green leaves till its snaky arms look like wands of green fur, each one tipped with a long finger of pure scarlet.

10

4

18

It is big country—clean country—and if it has no tenderness, it has strength and a sort of magnificence.

9
16a

To live there has always been a risky business—a matter not only of long chances and short shrifts but also of privation and danger. This was true of the prehistoric cave dwellers who lived only a little better than their animal neighbors in the Huecos many centuries gone by. It was true of the little pueblo communities

16 *and* 5
(*Note repetition
of "true" in
parallel
construction
here*)

which grew up later in the mountain canyons and wherever a wet-weather lake made existence possible on the valley floor. It was true in historic times of the peaceful Christian Indians who abandoned their unfinished church at Gran Quivira when the Apaches overwhelmed them nearly three hundred years ago.

Yes, it has always been hard country—frontier country—and for obvious reasons, the first reason being those same Apaches. The slopes of the Sierra Blanca were their favorite haunts as far back as we have any records, and though they ranged far and wide over the desert and even moved to Mexico for decades when the Comanches descended upon them, they always came back to the mountain rivers and the tall pines. A merciless environment made them tough and almost unbeatable fighters. They kept their country to themselves as long as they were able, waging a never-ending war against hunger and thirst, Comanches and Mexicans, soldiers and settlers, until their power was broken less than a lifetime ago.

Highways and railroads were slow in coming to a region so far removed from the gathering places of men and money. Sheer isolation did what the Apache was not able to do alone: it held off the traders and developers for years while the Rio Grande and Pecos settlements were booming.

But the most potent force of all for keeping people out was plain, old-fashioned, skin-cracking drought. The rainfall was imperceptible, and there was just enough ground water available to cause trouble. On the valley floor there was next to none at all until men got around to drilling wells. A few springs existed here and there in the Organs and the San Andres, none of them big enough to supply more than a few men and beasts. The eastern mountains were higher and better supplied. Spring-fed streams came down from the

9
9 and 18

12 and 5

17
3

4

14

Sierra Blanca at Three Rivers, while Tularosa Creek
descended the pass between Sierra Blanca and
Sacramento beside the main trail from the Pecos to the
Rio Grande.

Farther south, where the mile-high cliffs of the   13
Sacramentos soar above the plain, a number of
canyons drained off the water from the heights—Dog   10a
Canyon and Agua Chiquita; Sacramento and   5
Grapevine. In Sacramento Canyon and in Dog Canyon   14
the water was more or less permanent. But every-
where, until the skill and cupidity of man turned the   13
liquid gold to account, it flowed out onto the flats a
pitifully short distance and disappeared in the sand.
Along with it, as the years passed, flowed the blood of   15a
many a man who gave up his life for a trickle of water

Sensible men, cautious men, stayed away from   9a
such a place. But the adventurous and the hardy and   4a
the reckless kept on coming. Each one had a dream of
some sort—water for his cows, solitude for his soul,   4
gold to make him rich. For even the Tularosa country
has its treasures. The ghostly ruins of Gran Quivira
have been honeycombed by men obsessed with the
notion that the Indians buried a hoard of gold before
they left. At the northeast corner of the valley, in the   14
Jicarilla Mountains, lies the abandoned gold camp of
White Oaks, the site of rich mining properties seventy   15a
years ago. Midway between El Paso and Alamogordo,
on the rocky slopes of the Jarillas, Orogrande sits soli-
tary, remembering the days when prospectors and min-   12
ers swarmed in; and a few miles away at the San
Augustin Pass the abandoned shafts at Organ tell a
similar tale.

But the real story of Tularosa is the story of Texas
cattlemen—drifting herdsmen who began to invade the   10a
valley in the early eighties, bringing their stern folk-   12
ways with them. They too ran into trouble, for their

SENTENCE PATTERNS

law was not the law of the Mexicans or the Indians or 4a
the Yankees who arrived during and after the Civil Note parallel "it was"
War. It was those proud riders who kept the Old West construction
alive in that lonely land until yesterday. It was the
clash of their ways and standards with the ways and
standards of the settled citizens which caused the feuds 9
and killings and hatreds that make up the unwritten 4a
history of the region. The Apaches and the climate and
the lay of the land helped. But in the last analysis it 4a
was the Texans who made Tularosa the Last of the
Frontier West.

Those times seem as remote from present-day
reality as the wars of Caesar and Charlemagne, but
they have left a brand on the soul of many a man and
woman still living. That is why this story has never
been fully told—why all of it can never be told. For 17
out here in the desert the West of the old days has 9a
never quite given way to a newer America. Customs
have changed, but attitudes have held fast. To test this
fact, try asking questions about certain people and
events. Old men clam up and change the subject.
Young ones who have heard something hesitate a long
time before telling what they know about the sins and
tribulations of their grandfathers. Once it was dangerous to talk about these things. Even now it is not considered wise. The fears and loyalties and customs of 19
yesterday—these things still cast their shadows on us 19
who live on the edge of the desert. On the streets of El
Paso or Las Cruces or Alamogordo you can still hear 6
the click of bootheels belonging to men who played
their parts in dramas which would make a Hollywood 14 and 4a
movie look tame. Their sons and daughters still live
among us—fine people, too—and their friends still 7a
frown on loose discussion.

For these reasons this is not an easy story to tell, 14
but it is time someone told it. So let's go back to the

beginning, before the Texas cattle crowded in, ate the grass down to the roots, and trampled the plain into dust—back to the days when the country was the way   9
God made it: bunch grass growing up to a horse's belly; miles of yellow flowers in the wet years; little rainwater lakes at the foot of the Organs and the San   4
Andres, long since dried out and buried in dust; sun   12
and sand and sixty long miles to town.   4a

EXCERPT FROM *A THOUSAND DAYS**

Arthur M. Schlesinger, Jr.

SENTENCE
PATTERNS

After Kennedy's death, Adlai Steveson called him
the "contemporary man." His youth, his vitality, his
profound modernity—these were final elements in his
power and potentiality as he stood on the brink of the
Presidency. For Kennedy was not only the first
President to be born in the twentieth century. More
than that, he was the first representative in the White
House of a distinctive generation, the generation which
was born during the First World War, came of age during the depression, fought in the Second World War
and began its public career in the atomic age.

14
4 and 9a
6

9

This was the first generation to grow up as the
age of American innocence was coming to an end. To
have been born nearly a decade earlier, like Lyndon
Johnson, or nearly two decades earlier, like Adlai
Stevenson, was to be rooted in another and simpler
America. Scott Fitzgerald had written that his contem-
poraries grew up "to find all Gods dead, all wars
fought, all faiths in man shaken." But the generation
which came back from the Second World War found
that gods, wars, and faiths in man had, after all, survived if in queer and somber ways. The realities of the
twentieth century which had shocked their fathers now
wove the fabric of their own lives. Instead of reveling
in being a lost generation, they set out in one mood or
another to find, if not themselves, a still point in the
turning world. The predicament was even worse for the
generation which had been too young to fight in the
war, too young to recall the age of innocence, the generation which had experienced nothing but turbulence.
So in the fifties some sought security at the expense of
identity and became organization men. Others sought
identity at the expense of security and became beat-

11
11

9a
4

14

9a
9

*Note parallel
construction*

---

niks. Each course created only a partial man. There
was need for a way of life, a way of autonomy,
between past and present, the organization man and the
anarchist, the square and the beat.

    It was autonomy which this humane and self-suf-
ficient man seemed to embody. Kennedy simply could
not be reduced to the usual complex of sociological
generalizations. He was Irish, Catholic, New England,
Harvard, Navy, Palm Beach, Democrat, and so on; but
no classification contained him. He had wrought an
individuality which carried him beyond the definitions
of class and race, region and religion. He was a free
man, not just in the sense of the cold-war cliché, but in
the sense that he was, as much as man can be, self-
determined and not the servant of forces outside him.

    This sense of wholeness and freedom gave him
an extraordinary appeal not only to his own generation
but even more to those who came after, the children of
turbulence. Recent history had washed away the easy
consolations and the old formulas. Only a few things
remained on which contemporary man could rely, and
most were part of himself—family, friendship,
courage, reason, jokes, power, patriotism. Kennedy
demonstrated the possibility of the new self-reliance.
As he had liberated himself from the past, so he had
liberated himself from the need to rebel against the
past. He could insist on standards, admire physical
courage, attend his church, love his father while dis-
agreeing with him, love his country without self-doubt
or self-consciousness. Yet, while absorbing so much of
the traditional code, his sensibility was acutely con-
temporaneous. He voiced the disquietude of the post-
war generation—the mistrust of rhetoric, the disdain
for pomposity, the impatience with the postures and
pieties of other days, the resignation to disappoint-
ment. And he also voiced the new generation's long-

19

9
5

5
16

16

10a
4

16

4 (verbatim
series)

10a

4

ings—for fulfillment in experience, for the subordina-
tion of selfish impulses to higher ideals, for a link
between past and future, for adventure and valor and   *4a*
honor. What was forbidden were poses, histrionics, the
heart on the sleeve and the tongue on the cliché. What   *parallel construction
with pattern*
was required was a tough, nonchalant acceptance of   *17*
the harsh present and an open mind toward the
unknown future.

    This was Kennedy, with his deflationary war-time
understatement (when asked how he became a hero, he
said, "It was involuntary. They sank my boat"); his
contempt for demagoguery (once during the campaign,   *19*
after Kennedy had disappointed a Texas crowd by his
New England restraint, Bill Attwood suggested that
next time he wave his arms in the air like other politicians; Kennedy shook his head and wrote—he was
saving his voice—"I always swore one thing I'd never   *1*
do is—" and drew a picture of a man waving his arms
in the air); his freedom from dogma, his appetite for   *4*
responsibility, his instinct for novelty, his awareness   *and*
and irony and control; his imperturbable sureness in   *4a*
his own powers, not because he considered himself
infallible, but because, given the fallibility of all men,
he supposed he could do the job as well as anyone else;   *16*
his love of America and pride in its traditions and
ideals.

Time named Charles Kuralt "the laureate of the common man." He has the poet's gift for describing the infinite diversity of America and Americans. As you read the essay that follows, become aware of his passion for his subject and the grace and effortlessness of his style. Think about how Kuralt blends a variety of rhetorical tools into the paragraphs, matching and coordinating his rhetoric with his troubled message.

1. Analyze Kuralt's paragraphs and try to identify familiar sentence patterns. In particular, look for combinations of other sentence patterns.

2. Next, look for patterns that appeal to you. Try to imitate some of them and adapt them to your own writing.

3. Pay close attention to the vivid images Kuralt creates in his vivid language. Note how the immediacy of his descriptions makes historical figures come to life.

PLACE OF SORROWS*
(Little Big Horn, Montana)

Charles Kuralt

This is about a place where the wind blows and the grass grows and a river flows below a hill. Nothing is here but the wind and the grass and the river. But of all the places in America, this is the saddest place I know.

The Indians called the river the Greasy Grass. White men called it the Little Big Horn. From a gap in the mountains to the east, Brevet Major General George A. Custer's proud Seventh Cavalry came riding, early in the morning of June 25th, 1876, riding toward the Little Big Horn.

Custer sent one battalion, under Major Marcus Reno, across the river to attack what he thought might be a small village of hostile Sioux. His own battalion he galloped behind the ridges to ride down on the village from the rear. When at last Custer brought his two hundred and thirty-one troops to the top of a hill and looked down toward the river, what he saw was an encampment of fifteen thousand Indians stretching for two and a half miles, the largest assembly of Indians the plains had ever known—and a thousand mounted warriors coming straight for him.

Reno's men, meantime, had been turned, routed, chased across the river, joined by the rest of the regiment, surrounded, and now were dying, defending a nameless brown hill.

In a low, protected swale in the middle of their narrowing circle, the one surviving doctor improvised a field hospital and did what he could for the wounded. The grass covers the place now and grows in the shallow rifle trenches above, which were dug that day by knives and tin cups and fingernails.

Two friends in H Company, Private Charles Windolph and Private Julian Jones, fought up here, side by side, all that day, and stayed awake all that night, talking, both of them scared. Charles Windolph said: "The next morning when the firing commenced, I said to Julian, 'We'd better get our coats off.' He didn't move. I looked at him. He was shot through the heart." Charles Windolph won the Congressional Medal of Honor up here, survived, lived to be ninety-eight. He didn't die until 1950. And never a day passed in all those years that he didn't think of Julian Jones.

---

* Reprinted by permission of The Putnam Publishing Group from *On the Road with Charles Kuralt* by Charles Kuralt. Copyright © 1985 by CBS, Inc.

And Custer's men, four miles away? There are stones in the grass that tell the story of Custer's men. The stones all say the same things: "U.S. soldier, Seventh Cavalry, fell here, June 25, 1876."

The warriors of Sitting Bull, under the great Chief Gall, struck Custer first and divided his troops. Two Moon and the northern Cheyenne struck him next. And when he tried to gain a hilltop with the last remnants of his command, Crazy Horse rode over that hill with hundreds of warriors and right through his battalion.

The Indians who were there later agreed on two things: that Custer and his men fought with exceeding bravery; and that after half an hour, not one of them was alive.

The Army came back that winter—of course, the Army came back—and broke the Sioux and the Cheyenne and forced them back to the starvation of the reservations and, in time, murdered more old warriors and women and children on the Pine Ridge Reservation than Custer lost young men in battle here.

That's why this is the saddest place. For Custer and the Seventh Cavalry, courage only led to defeat. For Crazy Horse and the Sioux, victory only led to Wounded Knee.

Come here sometime, and you'll see. There is melancholy in the wind and sorrow in the grass, and the river weeps.

APPENDIX

Punctuation

Why punctuate?

Long association with the printed page has made most readers expect certain signals to conform to standard conventions.

denrael evah lla dluoc eW
sdrawkcab sdrow daer ot
tes dah sretnirp ylrae fi
yaw taht epyt rieht

˙llɐ ʇɐ ʞɔıɹʇ ou ʎllɐǝɹ sı uʍop-ǝpısdn
ƃuıpɐǝɹ ʇɐɥʇ puıɟ ǝldoǝd ʇsoɯ puɐ

Also, we know the shapes of printed words so well that

we can read almost anything when only the tops of letters show

but we have more difficulty when we can see only the bottoms.

The same kind of training has made us come to expect that printed words today will have spaces between them even though in many early writings   allthewordsrantogetherwithoutspacesanywherenotevenbetweensentencesandthereweerenosuchthingsasparagraphs.

In the same way, we expect that punctuation will follow conventions just as we expect to read from left to right and to find spaces between words so do we also expect the marks of punctuation to signal to us something about the relationships of words to each other after all the same arrangement of words for example Joe said Henry is a dirty slob can have two different meanings depending on the punctuation even a few marks to signal the end of each sentence would have helped you in this paragraph to help your reader give him some of the conventional signals we call punctuation marks.

Format for this page was partly suggested by John Spradley's article—"The Agenwit of Inpoint"—in JETT (*Journal of English Teaching Techniques*), Spring, 1971, pages 23–31.

Punctuation: a signal system

In the American English sentence, punctuation functions as a code, a set of signal systems for the readers to which they will respond. If your code is clear, the reader will get your signals. If your code is faulty, the reader will be confused and you will have failed to communicate. Some marks guide the eye; others, the ear, that is, they indicate the mental intonation (pause, stress, pitch) the reader should use. For instance, the period signals a full stop with pitch of voice dropped to indicate a long pause, whereas an exclamation point "shouts" at the reader and implies the raising of the writer's voice. The period indicates a long pause, whereas the comma indicates a short one. The semicolon signals not only a stop but also "equality": something equally structured will follow. The colon signals that the thought is not complete, that something explanatory will follow: an important word, phrase, sentence, or a formal listing. The colon is a very formal mark, whereas the dash is less formal, and material within parentheses just "whispers" to the reader. Generally speaking, these marks are not interchangeable; each has its own function to perform. It is important, therefore, that you learn when to use the following punctuation marks:

COLON: to call attention to what follows

1. before a list that follows a complete statement

Sara bought several items for her upcoming cruise: a two-piece bikini, a cocktail dress, and two pairs of metallic sandals.

2. before an independent clause that restates in different form the idea of the preceding independent clause (in a compound sentence)

A lizard never worries about losing its tail: it can always grow another.

3. after the words "following," "as follows," or "thus"

On her trip Sara planned to take the following: the newest Tom Clancy thriller, her brother's Nikon camera, and a stuffed cosmetic case.

4. before a climactic appositive at the end of the sentence

The grasping of seaweeds reveals the most resourceful part of the sea horse: it prehensile tail.

SEMICOLON: to separate important sentence elements

1. between independent clauses in a compound sentence without a conjunction

   Caesar, try on this toga; it seems to be your size.

2. between independent clauses in a compound sentence with a conjunction when there are commas in one or both clauses

   Sara has received an invitation to the Spanish ambassador's reception; she looks forward to dancing, but she will be disappointed if she can't try out the salsa, flamenco, or merengue.

3. before transitional connectives (conjunctive adverbs: *however, therefore, furthermore, thus, hence, likewise, moreover, nonetheless, nevertheless*) separating two independent clauses

   The race riot brought no peace to the city; nonetheless, it did force groups who had resisted before to talk to one another.

4. between items in a series containing internal commas

   Sara planned to take the following on her cruise: the newest Tom Clancy thriller, for five weeks the top best seller; her brother's camera, an expensive 35-millimeter Nikon; three garment bags, each filled with the very latest fashions; and plenty of greenbacks.

COMMAS: to separate main sentence elements

1. between independent clauses joined by coordinating conjunctions (*and, or, but, nor, for, yet, so*)

   I escaped from the burning house, but I lost many dear treasures from the past.

2. between elements of a series

   The produce counter had several varieties of lettuce, such as butter, romaine, red tip, and iceberg.

3. between contrasted elements in a "this, not that" construction

   The hostage seemed smug and defiant about his despicable act, neither sorry nor repentant.

4. before direct quotations (such constructions as *he said, she answered,* etc.)

   The politician said, "Yes, you must pay more taxes for Social Security."

5. between elements in dates, addresses, place names

Our new house is at 18 Denning Road, Hampstead, London NW 31SU England.

6. after a long introductory phrase or an adverbial clause preceding the main clause

If I buy too many municipal bonds, I may have less capital once interest rates begin to rise.

7. before an inverted element

The Tin Lizzie may have been dependable, but quiet it wasn't.

8. after any element that might be misread or might otherwise seem to run together

Once inside, the dog began to jump and bark.

9. in place of omitted words in elliptical constructions

A red light means stop; a green light, go.

10. after an absolute construction at the beginning of a sentence; before an absolute construction at the end

She sank back on her bed, her eyes filling with tears, her mouth grimacing in pain.

COMMAS: a pair to enclose

1. any interrupting construction between subject and verb, verb and object or complement, or any other two elements not normally separated

The weight of the prize-winning marlin, give or take a few ounces, was about 126 pounds.

2. a short appositive

The largest California vintner, the Gallo Company, has begun producing a new boutique wine, a Cabernet.

3. a noun or pronoun of direct address

Hey, you, get out of my way!

4. a nonrestrictive *(not* essential) interrupting modifier

Trisha's Victorian apartment, which I rented last summer, had mice in the pantry.

5. an absolute construction within a sentence

A break in the weather, God willing, is expected next week.

6. any parenthetical expression within a sentence

The understudy for the role, on the other hand, wanted as much money as the star.

DASH: to separate sentence elements

1. before a summary word to separate an introductory series of appositives from the independent clause

Dracula, Superman, Frankenstein's monster—all of these characters wore unusual costumes.

2. before an emphatic appositive at the end of a sentence

The grasping of seaweeds reveals the most resourceful part of the sea horse—its prehensile tail.

3. occasionally before a repetition for emphasis

The plumber came into the kitchen loaded—loaded with tools, not beer.

DASH: a pair to enclose

1. an internal series

Three basic fencing moves—the advance, the retreat, the lunge—demand careful balance by both fencers.

2. an abrupt change in thought or a pronounced sentence interrupter

Bill's wife—oh, whatever is her name?—brought a cherry pie to the picnic.

3. a parenthetical element, often for emphasis

Her recent behavior—however bizarre—must be judged with compassion.

4. an interrupting modifier or appositive for dramatic effect

Clancy's popular novel—*Hunt for Red October,* atop the best seller list for weeks—became a popular film.

PARENTHESES: a pair to enclose

1. words, phrases, expressions, or complete sentences that have no bearing upon the main idea (to make asides or "whispers" to the reader)

   I told Alice (who wouldn't?) the truth.

2. an interrupting series

   The colors of the flag (red, white, and blue) lavishly decorated the convention center.

3. an appositive

   His former wife (once a famous Philadelphia model) now owns a well-known boutique in the Bahamas.

4. an interrupting modifier between subject and verb

   The slogan of the state (comical yet enticing) helps promote tourism and a cleaner environment.

PERIOD:

1. at the end of a declarative sentence

   I enjoy creating new sentence patterns.

2. after an abbreviation

   CAUTION: Remember to put periods after abbreviations, such as Mr., etc., and Aug.

   In elementary school, children learn to use periods after common abbreviations: Mr., Mt., etc., St., and P.M.

3. to indicate an ellipsis (three spaced periods)

   The fourth graders raced through "I pledge allegiance . . . with liberty and justice for all" in thirty seconds.

QUESTION MARK:

1. at the end of a direct question

   Did you see that rose tattoo on Tommy's arm?

2. after each question in a series

Where are the jewels? the crown? the rings? the tiaras?

3. in parentheses to express uncertainty

In 742 (?) Charlemagne was born.

NOTE: Don't use a question mark to indicate

a. intended irony: His humorous letter failed to amuse her.

b. an indirect question: Joe asked when we were going to have chiles rellenos again.

c. a courteous request: Will you please pass the butter.

EXCLAMATION POINT:

1. after a phrase or sentence expressing intense emotion

"So what!" Eric yelled contemptuously.

2. after a strong interjection

Shut the door, you damned fool!

QUOTATION MARKS:

1. ALWAYS AFTER periods and commas

"I am not European," she said indignantly; "I am a U.S. citizen."

2. ALWAYS BEFORE colons and semicolons

Read James Joyce's short story "Araby"; learn what it's like to be disappointed in love.

Laura won an unexpected prize for her science-fair project, "Lumitox and the Environment": an all-expense-paid trip to Stockholm to attend the Nobel Prize ceremonies.

3. before or after question marks and exclamation points, depending upon the context of the sentence

James asked, "Can you meet me at seven o'clock?"

Did James say, "Meet me at seven o'clock"?

4. to enclose the actual words of a speaker

"Ask not what your country can do for you; ask what you can do for your country."

5. To identify symbols, letters, and words used as such

(He had too many "buts" in this paragraph, and his "$" sign is a simple "s.")

NOTE: In type, a word used as such is usually set in italics: too many *buts.*

6. to enclose the titles of short stories, short poems, paintings, songs, magazine articles, essays, and chapters of books, BUT NOT book titles

The subject matter of William Butler Yeats's "Leda and the Swan" and Correggio's painting "Leda" dramatize an erotic event that ultimately led to the Trojan war.

NOTE: In type the titles of works of art are often set in italic: Correggio's painting *Leda.*

BRACKETS:

1. to enclose additions, corrections, or other changes made in original quoted material

"Henry's traffic ticket in London cost him fifteen pounds [$30]," Molly had written in her diary.

2. to alert the reader to an error in quoted material. Use brackets around the Latin term *sic* (meaning "so" or "thus") to indicate the error in the quoted passage, such as an incorrect name, date, or spelling.

"Because Meryl was trying to loose [*sic*] weight, she was to [*sic*] ill to go to the wedding," Jim wrote in his letter.

The United States Postal Service now requires standardized addressing forms that can be scanned by computers and thus move the mail faster and more reliably. These new forms challenge traditional punctuation protocols by omitting commas and periods. Here are the six guidelines for standardized addressing:

1. Always put the addressee's name on the first line. (If you are sending mail to someone at a company, put the company name on the second line.)

2. In addition to the street address or post office box number, include the following if appropriate:

   N (North), S (South), E (East), W (West), NE, NW, SE, SW

3. Use the following abbreviations: AVE (Avenue), ST (Street), DR (Drive), RD (Road), PL (Place), CIR (Circle), BLVD (Boulevard), CT (Court), RM (Room), STE (Suite), or APT (Apartment) number.

4. Put the zip code after the city and state and on the same line. If you know the ZIP + 4 code, use it.

5. Capitalize and left-justify all lines. Do not punctuate.

6. Always include the return address.

Suggested review questions

PATTERN NUMBERS	
1 and 3	**1.** Explain the difference between a compound sentence with a semicolon and one with a colon. What is the specific difference in the second clause?
2	**2.** What kind of verb must be "understood" in the second clause before you can omit it?
	Can you ever omit something other than the verb in an elliptical construction?
4–8	**3.** What kinds of things can be listed in series?
	What slots in the sentence can contain series?
	Explain the patterns and the punctuation for the different kinds of series.
	4. In PATTERN 6, what two things come immediately after the series of appositives?
	5. Why must the series in PATTERN 7 be set off by a pair of dashes?
	What other marks of punctuation might occasionally substitute for those dashes?
	6. In what two particular places in an essay would PATTERN 8 be good to use? What should go into the dependent clause?
	7. What other patterns can perform the same function?
9	**8.** What qualifications should a word have before you put it in PATTERN 9?
9a	**9.** What kinds of words can you repeat in parallel structure? In what slots might they appear?
9	**10.** What kind of construction must come after the comma to keep PATTERN 9 from becoming a pattern 1 with a comma splice?
10 and 10a	**11.** Write one sentence three times, using different punctuation marks before the appositive (comma,

dash, colon). Then explain the difference in emphasis that the punctuation creates. Which is least emphatic? Which is most emphatic? Which makes a longer pause? Which is most formal?

12. What besides a single word can be an appositive?

13. *a.* What is the difference between the construction following the colon in PATTERN 3 and the one following the colon in PATTERN 10?

b. What is the difference between the construction following the dash in PATTERN 9 and the one following the dash in PATTERN 10a?

7a and 11

14. Explain the difference between an internal appositive and an interrupting modifier.

11

15. In PATTERN 11, what two main parts of the sentence are separated by the interrupting modifier?

11

16. What three marks of punctuation can separate an interrupting modifier from the rest of the sentence? Can you ever use just ONE of these marks?

17. Write the same sentence three times. Punctuate it with a pair of commas, a pair of dashes, and a pair of parentheses; then explain the difference in sound and emphasis in each.

11a

18. Write a sentence that functions as an interrupting modifier in another sentence.

11a

19. Write a question as an interrupting modifier. Where does the question mark go?

12

20. Where do participles come from? How are they always used? What different kinds of endings may the have?

12

21. How can you avoid a dangling participle in PATTERN 12?

13

22. What kind of modifier needs a comma after it in PATTERN 13?

PATTERN
NUMBERS

14	**23.** What does "inverted sentence" mean?
15	**24.** What purpose might lead you to invert a sentence?
15	**25.** What items in the normal order of a sentence may come out of their normal place (i.e., be inverted)?
15a	**26.** What cautions must you observe to make your inversions successful?
16	**27.** What kind of phrases (words) always come in pairs?
16	**28.** What kind of structures will PATTERN 16 help you join?
17	**29.** What kind of "signal words" begin dependent clauses that may function as subject or object or complement?
	30. Write two sentences using the same dependent clause. In one sentence, made the dependent clause the subject; in another, make it the direct object.
18	**31.** Describe an absolute construction; name its two parts. Can it ever be a complete sentence?
18	**32.** What is the difference between PATTERN 18 and the one with an introductory or concluding modifier?
18	**33.** If the absolute construction occurs in the middle of the sentence, what must your punctuation be?
18	**34.** Can absolute constructions ever occur in pairs or in series?
19	**35.** What is the difference between PATTERN 19 and the ordinary kind of short sentence?
19	**36.** What special functions can this pattern perform?
19	**37.** Why is the sound of this pattern so important? the rhythm? the context?
19a	**38.** What special functions can the short question perform?
19a	**39.** What are the two types of questions?

PATTERN
NUMBERS
19a

40. Where are good places to use a short question in writing?

20

41. What two reasons may make a writer use a deliberate fragment?

20

42. What is the importance of the surrounding context for a deliberate fragment?

20

43. What different kinds of functions may the fragment perform?

MISCELLANEOUS QUESTIONS (for class discussion or essay tests)

44. Write the same sentence twice and punctuate it two different ways. Discuss the difference in sound, emphasis, and effect.

45. Write a sentence with S—V—DO. Now put the DO in a different place and notice the effect.

46. Discuss how the same idea can be expressed with different kinds of phrasing, as in the following examples:

> Bad grades bother John.
> What bothers John is bad grades.
> John is bothered by bad grades.
> John, bothered by bad grades, decided to burn some midnight oil.
> Bad grades bothering John?
> Bad grades having bothered him before, John determined that this semester would be different.

47. Make up some sentences with nonsense words and discuss the structure and punctuation involved.

48. Define certain terms that occur in CHAPTER 2: *elliptical, appositive, parallel, construction, participle, absolute construction, series, modifier.*

49. What function does punctuation play in most sentences?

50. Why are style and variety in your sentence structure so important?